THE REAL-LIFE MYSTERY OF SHAKESPEARE'S LOST YEARS

Solving the Mysteries, Myths, & Mistakes of William Shakespeare

ROBERT BOOG

Copyright © 2023 Robert Boog

All rights reserved.

ISBN: **978-0-9666130-4-9**

DEDICATION

To Roxana, Brandon, Kevin, Juanito, Daisy. A debt of gratitude to the brilliant author J. Thomas Looney and my best friend Jim Behan. Also a shout out to my family: Gary & Jackie Kipka, Pat, Kevin, Margo & Mark, Paula & Randy, Tom, Sean & Vica, and Rosie. Finally thanks to people all over the world who question things and bother to ask "why"?

TABLE OF CONTENTS

INTRODUCTION 1
1 The Myth of Gaining a Patronage 4
2 The Mystery of Venus & Adonis 12
3 Marlowe's Mystery 17
4 The Mansion Myth 23
5 He 'Grew up in Town' Myth 29
6 The Two Maidenheads Mystery 37
7 A Mistake About Anne Hathaway 42
8 Was "Small Latin" a Big Mistake? 49
9 The "Anyone Could Have Written the Plays" Error 55
10 The Queen's Mistake 61
11 'The Rape of Lucrece' Mystery 70
12 The Lucrece Mystery Explained 74
13 The Boxing Day 'Mistake' 84
14 The Clayton Loan Mystery 89
15 The Myth of Oxford's Bad Poetry 92
16 The Tempest Myth 104
17 The Thomas North Mystery 111
18 About Honor & Other Things 117
19 Proof for William Shakespeare 123
20 Final Thoughts 129
RESOURCES 144
ABOUT THE AUTHOR 145

INTRODUCTION

When it comes to the authorship of William Shakespeare, there are two sets of lost years. The first takes place from William's birth in 1564 until he turned 18 and got married. The second takes place from the ages of 25 to 30. These missing years are from 1589 to 1594.

What happened? Where did William Shakespeare go?

Also, why should this still be a mystery? Over four hundred years have passed since his death, but details of his life are still a hot mess. As this book will show, the Shakespeare authorship is filled with myths, mysteries, and mistakes. It has divided people into two camps: those who believe Shakespeare wrote the Shakespeare canon and those who don't. It's impossible to write about his lost years without mentioning it.

When it comes to Shakespeare of Stratford-upon-Avon, many do not care about the truth. They will die on this hill that William Shakespeare from Stratford *must* be the author. People who believe otherwise are snobs who cannot accept the facts. Plus, William Shakespeare is a good guy with a feel-good story. His father was fined for having a dung heap at his front door which shows that great writers can come from humble beginnings.

Could unearthing the true details of the lost years reveal a different story entirely? What if we find facts about his authorship that were deliberately left out? What if a portrait was carefully altered to hide a different author's identity? Will this new information cause people to change their minds or will they stay loyal?

English accents, for example, vary from region to region. A video on *YouTube* features a man from the East Midlands area, Warwickshire, detailing an experience he had with the difference of accents between himself and a friend. One of the reasons this video stands out is that Shakespeare grew up in Warwickshire. During the video, the man explains how he and a friend had enjoyed a good laugh one night because their pal from London could not comprehend a single word they were saying. Why? His East Midlander slang was so different from how Londoners talk. Now, if this is still happening right now, why would it not have occurred 400 plus years ago?

Think about it. How could William Shakespeare, a mucky peasant from the Midlands, walk 90 miles to London and lose his accent over night? His epic poem *Venus & Adonis* contains over 1,100 lines, but not one trace of his Midlands accent can be found. Yet the people of London loved the poem so much; the publisher reprinted it ten times.

But let's say you were a schoolteacher living in London today. A Midlander student who just recently transferred into your class submitted verses that showed no sign of his Midland upbringing whatsoever. Might you find this a little odd?

We will bravely ask these tough questions because most academics seem to want to sweep them under the rug. Most will say "we have extant plays from his lifetime with his name on the book cover. His house is open for tours, so the Shakespeare authorship question is settled".

It's almost as bad as the police in Los Angeles when they claim, "We have an African-American male in custody, so there is no need to look for anyone else." Really?

Many academics even declare that nothing new can be discovered about William Shakespeare. This is simply not true. I was today's date old when I learned from author Lena Cowen Orlin's 2021 book *The Private Life of William Shakespeare* that even though William owned the second largest house in town, he and his wife rented out rooms to random lodgers. No wonder why William Shakespeare bequeathed his second-best bed to his wife. Some random tenant might have snagged it.

Please note: Since these missing years have been a hot topic for over 400 years, I am going to use a different approach. I will be looking at these myths, mysteries, and mistakes from the view of an average Joe sleuth. I will jump forward and backward in time and hopefully, this will not be too confusing.

Also I will try to infuse this book with a little slang and a bit of humor. It is not going to be dull like that famous star in the sky with no sense of humor: Sirius.

Finally, I want you to join my quest. Think of it like joining a "cold case" investigation. You will be charged with looking into this case with fresh eyes. The question of William Shakespeare's authorship will no longer be considered "settled". Instead, we will leave everything open for debate and at the end you will decide for yourself.

Most scholars use footnotes, but I will offer links to websites instead so if you are interested, you can read the articles in their entirety. Those links will be found at the end of each chapter under the heading "Sources". Now, we will start by diving into deep waters starting with the year 1588. This year is key to understanding what William Shakespeare may have been doing during his lost years of 1589 to 1594.

Sources

The Shakespeare Documented Website:
https://shakespearedocumented.folger.edu/resource/family-legal-property-records

William Shakespeare: A Study of the Facts and Problems (2 vols, 1930).
https://www.google.com/books/edition/William_Shakespeare/F9X3zAEACAAJ?hl=en

1

The Myth of Gaining a Patronage

Lord Burghley

In 1588, most people would agree that Lord Burghley was the most powerful man living in England. But who was he? Lord Burghley's real name was William Cecil. He acted as chief advisor, treasurer, and right-hand man to Queen Elizabeth I.

Technically his title was Baron Burghley but that reminded me of Snoopy and the Red Baron so to keep things simple, I will refer to him as Lord Burghley. He is a major player in the Shakespeare authorship debate, but the average person is likely to have never heard of him.

In mid-June of 1588, the English Navy was about to engage in battle with the 150 ships of the Spanish Armada, but while this was happening, Lord Burghley had personal matters that filled his mind. His eldest daughter, Anne Cecil de Vere had died. Burghley sent an urgent message to Anne's husband, Edward de Vere, the 17th Earl of Oxford to return to London.

(Edward de Vere the 17th earl of Oxford is a long name and because I am lazy, I will refer to Edward de Vere as "Oxford.")

Upon returning home and learning that his 31 year old wife had perished, Oxford went on an extended drinking binge. The binge also including gambling, fornicating, behaving badly, and lavishly spending money. His behavior resembled more of a happy-go-lucky fraternity brother than of a grieving spouse.

Nowadays psychologists use jargon such as "self-medication" to describe how some may try to regulate their intense negative emotions through alcohol. These days a song about someone who drowns their sorrows in booze sounds almost like a cliché, but back in the late 1580s, most people would not understand why any husband would want to get drunk after losing his wife. They considered it a sign of uncaring. Or mental weakness. Or both.

Oxford's actions disgusted Lord Burghley, so much so, he demanded that he give up custody of his three daughters. Burghley believed his son-in-law was unfit to raise them, and Oxford agreed. So, Lord Burghley and his wife (the children's grandmother) moved the girls to Cecil House, a prominent mansion with a library of over 3,000 books where Oxford had grown up.

Oxford's eldest daughter, named Elizabeth Vere, was fourteen years old, smart as a whip, and beautiful. She turned heads with her dark eyes and raven-colored hair.

Also living at Cecil House was the dashing earl of Southampton, 16-year-old Henry Wriothesley, who at that time was one of the most eligible bachelors in England.

The two teens couldn't help but meeting in the large mansion and stealing glances. Lord Burghley took great delight in this as he approved their mutual interest. As legal guardian of both Henry Wriothesley and Elizabeth Vere, Lord Burghley quickly arranged for the two teens to marry.

Did her father, Edward de Vere want her to marry Henry? We do not know, but if Lord Burghley wanted them to marry and his son-in-law, Oxford, disagreed, might there have been some harsh words between the two men?

More important: Did William Shakespeare living in Stratford upon Avon know either one of these two lovebirds? It does not seem likely, but we will get to this in just a minute.

Under the legal age of 21, neither Henry nor Elizabeth had much say in arranging their futures. Nor did Elizabeth's father, Edward de Vere. He had given up his rights when he had allowed Lord Burghley and his wife to raise his three daughters.

Suppose one rainy night, Oxford had knocked on the doors of the mansion and told Lord Burghley, "I must speak to my daughter. I cannot and will NOT allow her to marry Henry Wriothesley."

"Yes. Well, she is asleep now, but I will see that she gets your message first thing in the morning," Lord Burghley reassures him. Then after he departs, Burghley tells his wife. "Oxford may wish to sabotage the nuptials. Please alert the staff that any letters from Edward de Vere should be brought to me immediately."

"Will you burn these letters?" his wife asks.

"Of course, I will burn them. Henry Wriothesley is the richest earl in all of England. His marriage to Elizabeth Vere must go through."

Lord Burghley did not believe in love. He once wrote that marriages should be based on political and economic issues, and he famously argued that "marriages of physical desire begin with happiness and end in grief."

Obviously, Burghley was a hopeless romantic.

By the way, when I was growing up, I was taught William Shakespeare wrote *Venus & Adonis* to obtain a patronage from Henry Wriothesley. Back then, I was told Henry was one of the richest earls in all of England.

Therefore, I imagined him to be in his late 50s like some weird dude with a comb-over and a beard. A beardo, right? I was not aware that the wealthiest man in all of England was only a sixteen-year-old boy about my same age. Like me he probably ate sadghetti (when you eat spaghetti alone and depressed).

Some months later, high-schooler Henry Wriothesley declined Lord Burghley's proposal, meaning he had refused a marriage proposal from the most powerful man in England. Henry claimed he was too young to get married and told his legal guardian to "shove it." When I learned about this, I whistled under my breath and thought, "Wow. This kid had balls."

Lord Burghley remained as cool as a cucumber but like many rich, hot-tempered people in Los Angeles who do not get their way, he threatened Henry with legal action. He told him, "If you fail to marry my granddaughter, Elizabeth Vere, then you must pay a huge fine that could potentially ruin you and your life forever!"

To which the boy replied, "Bring it, Lord Burghley. I have plenty of money. I will pay your fine."

Some people today might empathize with the young earl. Henry could not legally buy weed, and yet he was being forced to marry someone because it was seen as a smart business decision. Wait. This does not make sense. What had I been taught in school again?

Like most students, I was taught that William Shakespeare had no record of ever attending school. He lived in a small town but had no job skills. William had left his impoverished wife with three young children and hoofed it to London. Desperate for money, he wrote a 1,100-line poem called *Venus and Adonis* and dedicated it to Henry Wriothesley. He did this hoping to gain a patronage.

The story goes, the poem was published in 1593 and got reprinted ten times. It was a massive hit. Plays like *Romeo & Juliet* followed soon after that and William soon became rich.

But what if this tale was not entirely true? What if you and I were never actually told the *entire* story? I want to let you in on a little secret. Scholars left out some critical information.

Two years before *Venus and Adonis* came out, a poem called *Narcissus* was the talk of the Elizabethan court.

Dedicated to Henry Wriothesley, *Narcissus* concerned a handsome, fifteen-year-old Greek god named Narcissus who lived on a blessed island ruled by a Virgin Queen. Consumed only with love for himself, Narcissus lacked honor and virility. He died alone, sad, and without leaving any heirs. His vain, pathetic, egotistical behavior proved to be his fatal flaw.

It would not take Sherlock Holmes to deduce that *Narcissus* described the young Earl of Southampton, Henry Wriothesley, and his refusal to marry Elizabeth Vere.

Henry Wriothesley

The poem had attacked Henry Wriothesley's character because it implied that he lacked honor and was less than virile. And to be quite honest, sixteen-year-old Henry Wriothesley did style an effeminate look, especially because he wore his hair long. He may have been bisexual too, as his dashing good looks were said to charm both men and women.

Last in his bloodline, his surname would die with him if he failed to produce an heir. Siring a son was of great importance to people back then.

THE MYSTERY OF SHAKESPEARE'S LOST YEARS

Well, maybe important to everyone *but* Henry Wriothesley. He did not care if he got married or not. He believed he had plenty of time to find a wife and settle down. Did he truly lack virility and honor? No. That was a cheap shot.

This obscure poem did not come to light until 1991, perhaps because it was written in Latin. You can find an article about it written by Charles Martindale and Colin Burrow (see the Sources section at the end of this chapter.)

If you do decide to read the poem, you might want to focus on its tone. It comes off as a bit dull and moralizing. The author states, "you should do this but not that" quite often which after a while slows down the read. The poem talks about getting caught up in the selfish desires of beauty, and ego. It says that life presents many beautiful things to appreciate and do not lose sight of the beauty of marriage.

Certainly, getting married and having children can bring immense joy, but why would someone publicly humiliate the wealthiest earl in all of England? Did the poet personally know Henry Wriothesley?

The poet's name was John Clapham and he worked as a clerk. Still, does it not seem a little odd that a secretary would write a poem in Latin that attacked a young man's honor and virility? Especially if the earl's legal guardian was Lord Burghley? The most powerful man in all of England? Wouldn't you be afraid that Lord Burghley might come after you?

Spoiler Alert: If you Google the name "John Clapham" you will discover that John Clapham was Lord Burghley's secretary. But that is not all folks. There's more!

In the poem *Narcissus*, John Clapham's writing style matches Lord Burghley's. So, is it possible that Lord Burghley could have dictated the poem and like a dutiful lapdog, John Clapham wrote it all down?

This is what I believe happened.

In my opinion, even though John Clapham's name can be found on the title page, he did NOT actually pen *Narcissus*. Lord Burghley did. An expert in Latin, Burghley had the poem published obscurely to not completely humiliate the boy. After all, most of the population in England were illiterate and only the wealthiest and most literate people would buy and read books in Latin.

What is an Allonym?

Wikipedia defines "allonym" as a "ghostwriter." The Merriam-Webster dictionary defines "allonym" as "a name that is assumed by an author but that actually belongs to another person."

Having John Clapham listed as the author of *Narcissus* allowed Lord Burghley to retaliate at Southampton passively yet aggressively without getting his hands dirty. No one could ever accuse Lord Burghley of drafting a mean-spirited Latin poem because his name did not appear on its title page. Would people still shame the sixteen-year-old boy or make fun of him? Yes, but would that be such a terrible thing?

Not really. It would teach Henry Wriothesley a firm lesson about the importance of getting married as well as not to disrespect your elders.

But think about it. A 16-year-old boy had stood up to the most powerful man in England and survived. So, what happened next?

Two years later, *Venus & Adonis,* allegedly written by a mucky Midlander named William Shakespeare, whose father left a dung heap at his front door offered an elegant, poetic response to *Narcissus*.

Shakespeare experts tell us this poem has several things in common with *Narcissus*, and that Shakespeare tried to show up the author of Narcissus by writing an even better poem. *Venus & Adonis* was written in English and was twice as long. As mentioned before: it became a bestseller and the talk of the town. The question is, why? Why would William Shakespeare get involved in the middle of a public shaming of an earl?

A Brief Recap

Lord Burghley controlled Henry's finances and was angry with Henry Wriothesley for refusing his marriage proposal. So, would Lord Burghley make it easy for Henry Wriothesley to spend money? Think about it.

Sources

Midlands Accent on YT:
https://www.youtube.com/watch?v=227HtFru8To

Narcissus www.jstor.org/stable/4344790.

2

The Mystery of Venus & Adonis

Reading the dedication to *Venus & Adonis* one word jumps out at us. It is the word "honor" because Shakespeare uses it seven times. Honor means good name or public esteem: reputation and a showing of respect received from others.

> To the Right <u>Honorable</u> Henrie Wriothesley, Earle of Southampton, and Baron of Titchfield.
>
> Right <u>Honourable</u>,
>
> I know not how I shall offend in dedicating my unpolisht lines to your Lordship, nor how the worlde will censure mee for choosing so strong a proppe to support so weake a burthen, onelye if your <u>Honour</u> seeme but pleased, I account my selfe highly praised, and vowe to take advantage of all idle houres, till I have <u>honoured</u> you with some graver labour. But if the first heire of my invention prove deformed, I shall be sorie it had so noble a god-father: and never hereafter eare so barren a land, for feare it yeeld me still so bad a harvest, I leave it to your <u>Honourable</u> survey, and your <u>Honor</u> to your hearts content which I wish may alwaies answere your owne wish, and the worlds hopefull expectation.
>
> Your <u>Honors</u> in all dutie, William Shakespeare.

Venus & Adonis answered *Narcissus* and explained to the public how Adonis could be seen as being honorable. In the poem, he comes across like a young Christian youth resisting a sexy, older woman's advances, while Venus exudes cunning and experience. She seems like a modern woman filled with love, lust, and desire. She pursues him, and when Adonis gives in to her temptation, it seems like it was not entirely his fault. Venus had used her goddess-like charms on this 15-year-old boy.

Again, it would not take Sherlock Holmes to deduce that Adonis referred to Henry Wriothesley, and because *Venus & Adonis* shared several features in common with *Narcissus* by John Clapham, the author of *Venus & Adonis* must have read *Narcissus*. Not only that, but the author had tried to one-up him.

> Stable URL
> https://www.jstor.org/stable/43447390
>
> ABSTRACT
>
> The obscure neo-Latin poem Narcissus by John Clapham <u>was the first literary work to be dedicated to the Earl of Southampton, who was also to become the dedicatee of Shakespeare's Venus and Adonis</u>. The poem has several features in common with Shakespeare's (a vocal deity of love, a lustful horse, a short echo-poem), in comparison with which Shakespeare may well have sought to establish the superiority of his own work. It may also have helped to create a nexus of associations between the myth of Adonis and that of Narcissus, which runs through Shakespeare's early verse. The poem is here edited, annotated, and translated for the first time.

Why would a 29-year-old unemployed married man want to establish his superiority over another author? Honor was important to Elizabethans. Back then, insults to one's personal reputation had to be avenged as a matter of personal pride. So, if the author of *Narcissus* had felt disrespected, might not he want to challenge Shakespeare to a duel to avenge the loss of his good name?

Let us suppose that Henry Wriothesley was Shakespeare's patron. Henry paid William Shakespeare to write a poem to defend his honor. If so, Shakespeare would have first needed to read *Narcissus*. But how would William Shakespeare get paid if Lord Burghley controlled the boy's purse strings until he was 21? Scholars have searched high and low for letters and/or receipts between Henry and William to answer this question but have come up empty. No connection between the two appears to exist.

Instead, educators have long compelled students to memorize that Wriothesley acted as Shakespeare's patron. They have called it a "fact" even though absolutely no proof exists. Henry Wriothesley never even sent William Shakespeare a brief "thank you" note.

I do not blame teachers however, because like scholars of the past 400+ years, John Clapham's poem *Narcissus* had been kept hidden. The obscure poem was found only recently.

Therefore, do not feel bad if you too feel tricked. Scholars for the past 400 years ago were fooled too. But what do most people do once they have been duped? They tell someone, and that is why I am reaching out to you in the hope that you will do some personal research or ask your teachers or local Shakespeare expert about Clapham's poem.

Were you aware that *Venus & Adonis* ends with the death of Adonis? He gets gored by a wild boar and interestingly, a wild, blue boar sits atop the family crest of Edward de Vere. Perhaps this poem was a message from Oxford to Henry Wriothesley telling him *not* to marry his daughter?

Bouncing back to *Venus & Adonis*: What do you think Queen Elizabeth thought about this poem? Do you think she enjoyed the soft-porn aspects and how Adonis viewed the naked goddess?

Knowing Queen Elizabeth's vain and volatile temperament, she probably hated it. In fact, after reading *Venus & Adonis*, Queen Elizabeth probably exploded in a fit of rage. Why? She may have felt like someone was gaslighting her, because prior to this poem, her beauty had been compared to the goddess Venus. During her time in power, Elizabeth had tried hard to portray herself as the "Virgin" Queen. So, the idea of the Queen of England acting like a lusty cougar and chasing after a handsome young man who had first refused her advances might not have sat well with her. At all.

It's true. William Shakespeare's poem made Venus seem ~~slutty~~ less than dignified. The sexy goddess showed loose morals and little respect for others because of her self-centered point of view. It may have caused readers to pause, raise an eyebrow and scoff.

Lord Burghley had a problem. Not only had a sixteen-year-old boy disparaged him, but so had the author of *Venus & Adonis*. The author had emphasized the boy's honor and seemed to applaud him for resisting the arranged marriage. Even worse, his poem had made the queen look less than honorable. But why would William Shakespeare want to piss off the Queen?

Queen Elizabeth may have given Burghley a simple command: FIND HIM. What would Burghley do to the author once he found him? Take him out to lunch? I do not think so.

According to the website Historic-UK.com: The rack was Lord Burghley's favorite tool and the most widely used Elizabethan instrument of torture. Designed to stretch the victim's body, eventually dislocating the limbs, it would rip them from their sockets.

At the Tower of London, it was affectionately called the Duke of Exeter's Daughter, as it was claimed to be the invention of the Duke, a Constable of the Tower in the 15th century. The prisoner was shown the rack first and then questioned; only if the prisoner refused to answer was the rack used. It is known that the sheer sight of the rack was often enough for people to surrender and give up whatever information was wanted. So, whether William Shakespeare of Stratford upon Avon had authored the poem or not, Lord Burghley most likely would have wanted to have a chat with him.

Sources

Narcissus by John Clapham:
https://www.jstor.org/stable/43447390

The Atlantic Magazine Article The Case for Edward de Vere

De Vere family Coat of Arms

3

Marlowe's Mystery

Over the years, many people have believed that Christopher Marlowe wrote the Shakespeare canon.

Christopher Marlowe

Lord Burghley may have thought so too. Why? Thirty days after *Venus & Adonis* arrived in print, three drunken dinner-goers at the private house of Dame Eleanor Bull (not a public tavern) watched as Christopher Marlowe got stabbed, bled out and died. Official documents stated Marlowe had argued over the dinner bill, then pulled a dagger on businessperson Ingram Frizer, who retaliated by stabbing Christopher Marlowe through his left eye. Marlowe died instantaneously.

Frizer's "self-defense" part of the story seems sketchy because for several years, Christopher Marlowe had worked in some intelligence capacity on behalf of the British government. During the spring of 1593, he had stayed at the home of Thomas Walsingham, a relative of Francis Walsingham, the head of her majesty's secret service.

The dodgy characters Christopher Marlowe met the night of his assassination had associations to the secret service, so perhaps the attack may have been planned and, all three may have ganged up on him. We will never know what really happened that night, but we do know one fact: Francis Walsingham, the head of the secret service, answered to one man, Lord Burghley.

Known publicly to be an atheist, Christopher Marlowe was out on bail after being accused of heresy. He had stated publicly he did not believe in God, a crime punishable by burning at the stake. Due to the popularity of his plays, Christopher Marlowe had developed a large group of followers who were also atheists.

If Lord Burghley had told Walsingham that Christopher Marlowe's atheism was causing problems for the Queen or she wanted him dead, would his men have hesitated to kill him? I do not think so.

Lord Burghley passionately believed the interests of the state (including the established Anglican church) superseded the life of one individual. So, if Burghley believed a nonbeliever had blackened the reputation of good Queen Bess (who was head of the church of England) it seems unlikely Burghley would have stopped until he felt certain he had eradicated England of the atheist. They could not have mobs of nonbelievers challenging the rule of the queen.

Plus, Christopher Marlowe had written the play, *Dido Queen of Carthage* and in it, the queen of Carthage died for the love of Aeneas, a younger, mythical hero and son of the beautiful queen Aphrodite. It was another love story involving a powerful older woman and a younger man.

Writing plays for the theater required Christopher Marlowe to have a patron and Ferdinando Stanley acted as his main sponsor. He financed Christopher Marlowe's plays, and they were performed by Stanley's acting company which was known as Lord Strange's Men. They were the first acting company to perform Shakespeare's *Henry VI* plays.

What happened to Ferdinando Stanley? One year after Christopher Marlowe's death, a servant found him dead. Ferdinando Stanley had been poisoned. This happened in April 1594: one year after Christopher Marlowe's death and the person long suspected of being behind it? Lord Burghley. Naturally Burghley would not have done the deed himself. Francis Walsingham would have been summoned and he would have hired someone to do the dirty work.

Ferdinando Stanley

Most people today, including myself, will dismiss conspiracy theories about the government, but at this point in history it seems reasonable to believe that they did exist. Back then, government agents were known to have been involved in silencing political radicals.

Therefore, when people today claim that any noble person who penned poems and plays could have openly put his name on the title page, it is true, just as it is true that a person today can sell drugs openly on any street corner in L.A. It can be done, true, however, there might be consequences and police repercussions for doing so.

Lord Burghley came across as a very gentle, pious person who would not hurt a fly. But he was known to have a temper and was famous for using the rack.

Therefore, if there was nothing to fear by putting the real author's name on a play, then why were Christopher Marlowe and people close to Christopher Marlowe showing up dead? Thomas Kyd, the author of *The Spanish Tragedy,* the hottest play of its time, was arrested shortly after Marlowe's death. Both his rooms and offices were searched, allegedly for heretical material. What was his association to Christopher Marlowe? Thomas Kyd had once been his roommate. Care to guess *when* this happened? He was jailed in May of 1593, again, 30 days after the publication of *Venus & Adonis.*

Thomas Kyd lived only one more year before his premature death at age 36 in August 1594.

Most scholars agree that Thomas Kyd had endured weeks and maybe months of torture on Lord Burghley's rack.

The rack had broken him and led to Kyd's early demise. He could no longer use his hands to write.

Let us go back to William Shakespeare's missing years. If you were Richard Field, who had printed things for Lord Burghley and had heard rumors about his penchant for using the rack, would you suggest that your friend William Shakespeare show his face around London after the publication of *Venus & Adonis*? No. It was far too dangerous. Plus, hiding Shakespeare in your own house might put your family in danger as well.

Ever notice that Shakespeare's name does not show up on the title page of plays until *after* 1597? It is true. This is when Lord Burghley's health began to quickly decline. He died in 1598, but before 1597, the title pages of plays later attributed to William Shakespeare were blank. *Palladas Tamia* by Francis Meres, the first book to ever mention Shakespeare's name, came out in 1598 It arrived one month after Burghley's death.

Nevertheless, many people believe during the years from 1592 to 1594, William Shakespeare belonged to an acting company, and he freely toured the English countryside.

They tell us William Shakespeare "most likely" joined a company of players like Lord Strange's Men. Acting before crowds of people would have helped Shakespeare lose his Midlands accent. Although this conjecture makes sense, in real life, William Shakespeare went missing in action.

When acting companies went on tour, most small towns required the actors to sign their names in guest books. Today, the names of all the other actors can still be found, but NOT the name William Shakespeare.

THE MYSTERY OF SHAKESPEARE'S LOST YEARS

His name *has never been found* on any of these town ledgers. Why not? If William Shakespeare had traveled the country, why can't his name be found alongside the other actors of his time?

More than likely, from 1592 to 1594, William had holed up in his hometown. Like the head of the Gestapo, Lord Burghley had spies everywhere. So, if William Shakespeare was performing in front of audiences in London or the countryside, wouldn't he be eventually found out by Burghley's spies and brought in for questioning? It never happened.

Lord Burghley may have assumed that William Shakespeare was an allonym for Christopher Marlowe and that by killing the real Christopher Marlowe, he had silenced his pseudonym. William Shakespeare. Forever.

Venus & Adonis had been printed at the shop run by Richard Field. His father was a tanner who lived in Stratford upon Avon and knew William's father, so William Shakespeare may have known Richard growing up. If so, might William have stayed at Richard's house and read books at Richard Field's shop that Shakespeare later used to write some of his plays?

It makes sense; however, it seems somewhat risky. Richard Field's printing house was located only a stones-throw away from Lord Burghley's residence.

But the town of Stratford upon Avon? It would be completely off Lord Burghley's radar. Ninety miles away, or about the distance from Los Angeles to San Diego, it took three days by horse to journey from Stratford upon Avon to London. And that was without traffic.

Far safer for William Shakespeare to hang out with his wife and children. If Lord Burghley's men did find him in Shottery, he could tell them that his name was NOT William Shakespeare. He could even take them to the Holy Trinity Church to prove it. There he could show them that his father had baptized him as Guilielmus Shakspere.

A Brief Recap

Although some anecdotal claims exist that William Shakespeare may have engaged in an acting career after leaving his hometown of Stratford upon Avon, guestbook registers tell us a different story. William Shakespeare may have left Stratford, but most likely returned to Shottery to stay with his wife and three children until the coast was clear.

Sources

https://elizabethanenglandlife.com/christopher-marlowe-famous-elizabethan-writer/christopher-marlowe-death-the-conspiracy-theories.html

Henry Wriothesley and cat

4

The Mansion Myth

I have worked as a real estate broker and a notary public for over 30 years, meaning I have watched thousands of people sign documents. For a while the school district required parents to notarize a form stating that their child lived within the school boundaries. This got me to thinking about William Shakespeare and his grammar school education.

See, there are no records of him ever attending any school, yet experts claim he must have appeared in classes every day from 7:00 in the morning till 6:00 at night six days a week. But for this to happen, his parents would have needed to live in town within the school boundaries.

When it comes to our cold case mystery, I wanted to be 100% certain that William Shakespeare's father, John Shakespeare, *did* live in town. For centuries people have just assumed it. Here is where some people will smile and give me a big thumbs up. After all, there is a house near a grammar school in Stratford-upon-Avon called "the Shakespeare birthplace trust home." They give tours there daily about William Shakespeare.

But let us not assume anything. Instead, we shall rewind the clock to the year 1552, when William's father was 20 years old. Let us discover how the birthplace trust home came to be.

Scholars tell us that back in 1552, John Shakespeare and two other men were fined one shilling apiece for keeping a "muckheap" outside a house on Henley Street. Since the plague traveled by rats, the fine may have been intended to stop the spread of the disease. Old timers reasoned

the western half of the property in 1552 was 60 feet wide.

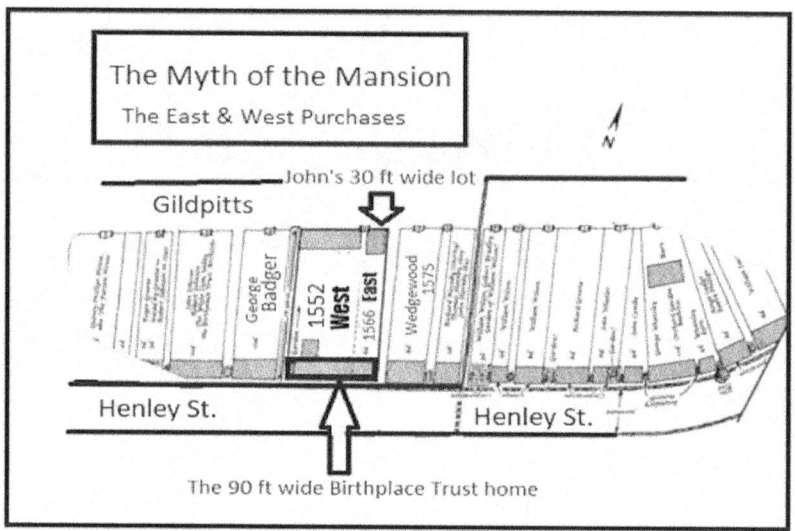

Then in 1556, John bought a 30-foot-wide property to the east. Joining the two lots together, John Shakespeare could now build a spacious mansion for William to be born in 1564. Unfortunately, the historical records show he only purchased **one** property on Henley Street.

Records show that in 1556, John Shakespeare purchased two tenements. One was on Greenhill Street and the other on Henley Street. Both were 30 to 35 feet wide, and they could have been two vacant lots because in those days, the word "tenement" was used freely to describe *any* real property.

"Tenement" comes from the Latin word "teneo" meaning "to hold" so although modern readers might imagine a row of houses or multi-level structures, this is not true. Back then, a tenement could mean a vacant lot or a dwelling. But there is no mention of John purchasing a 60 ft. wide property in 1552 when he was 20 years old.

His second purchase was of a house and garden in Henley Street which he bought from Edward West. This also carried the obligation of an annual chief rent of six pence, which indicates it had a street frontage of about 30-35

THE MYSTERY OF SHAKESPEARE'S LOST YEARS

The present-day Shakespeare Birthplace Trust home on Henley Street spans 90 feet wide, so how could John Shakespeare have built it on a 30 ft. wide lot? It is impossible.

Therefore, we know William Shakespeare was NOT born in a three-story mansion on Henley Street like the one that exists there today.

Our cold case mystery deepens. How did this rumor get started? Why would so many experts believe this to be the house where William Shakespeare was born?

Let us review by going backwards in time:

In 1597, John Shakespeare sold a sliver of property 1.5 feet wide by 84 feet long to George Badger.

Before this, in 1575, John's neighbor to the west of his property, Edmund Hall, sold a 61.5 ft wide property to John Shakespeare in 1575. This property had two houses on it.

Edmund Hall and his wife Emma offered to sell it to John Shakespeare because she had inherited it from her father, Edward West who had sold John his first property in 1566.

So, in 1575, John Shakespeare took Edmund Hall to court, which is how real estate was transacted. There were no friendly real estate agents - just a friendly lawsuit to purchase the Hall's property.

Two weeks before this happened, still in 1575, John had witnessed a deed for Mr. Wedgewood, his neighbor to the east. (To the **right** of the arrows.) On this document, John had the scribe add the word 'yeoman' next to his name, as John Shakespeare was illiterate, and signed his name with a mark.

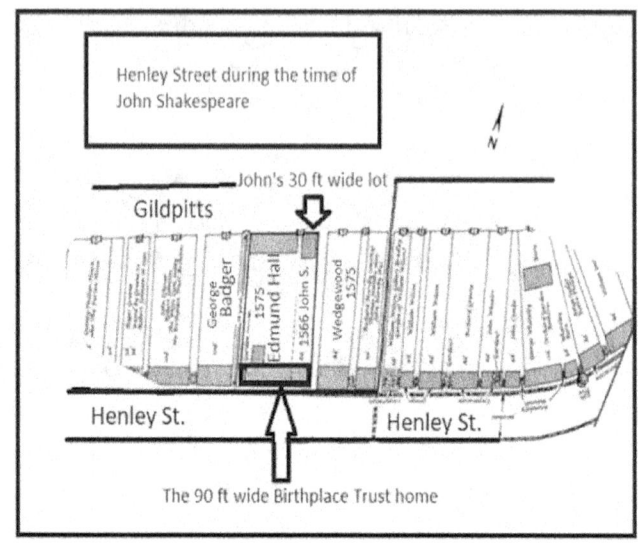

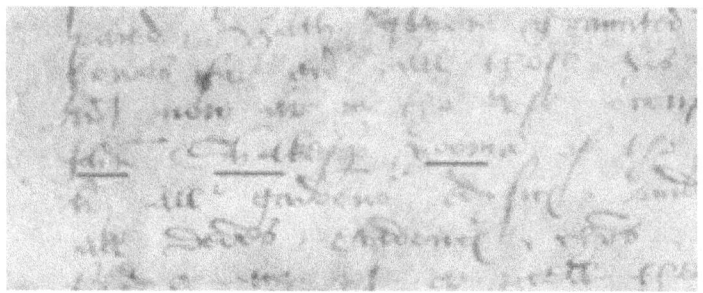

Do you see the word "yeoman" beside his name? It means "farmer". Remember, this happened in 1575, *nineteen years* after John Shakespeare first purchased the property on Henley Street in 1566. Nineteen years is a long time to wait to buy the property next door. But how does this help us ascertain whether John Shakespeare really raised his family in town?

In 1575, William Shakespeare would have been eleven years old, and his parents would have had five children.

The 61.5 ft wide property from Edmund and Emma Hall had two messuages (houses) on it, so John Shakespeare could have knocked them down to build a three-story mansion close to the grammar school. But he never did. The two houses had tenants and because John needed the money, he kept them as rentals. We know this because in 1582, one of his tenants, William Burbage took John Shakespeare to court.

Sadly, John Shakespeare passed away in 1601 without ever building a mansion on his Henley Street property. However, just two years later, William Shakespeare paid for a spacious 3-story mansion to be built on the property. Then he told everyone, "This is the house where I grew up."

Was William ashamed of his "real" home and wanted people to believe his father had raised him in a mansion, close to a school? Possibly. It may have convinced people that Will had attended the local grammar school, because it was only a couple of blocks from his father's place on Henley Street.

How does this relate to William Shakespeare's missing years? Although church records shows that a Guilielmus Shaksper was baptized at the Holy Trinity Church, there is no actual *written evidence* proving William Shakespeare grew up in the town of Stratford upon Avon. None. But there is written evidence that scholars have known about for over 100 years that shows John Shakespeare was a tenant of a farm located four miles outside of the village of Stratford upon Avon. We will talk more about this in the next chapter.

A Brief Recap

The present-day Shakespeare Birthplace Trust home on Henley Street spans 90 feet wide and was allegedly built to replicate the former home of John Shakespeare. But William's father could not have built a spacious mansion on the tiny lot he owned on Henley Street. It was not wide enough. He did not come into possession of the Hall's adjacent 61.5

ft. wide property until 1575.

Sources

Foot of Fine recording the conveyance of two messuages, two gardens and two orchards in Stratford-upon-Avon by Edmund Hall to John Shakespeare

https://shakespearedocumented.folger.edu/resource/document/foot-fine-recording-conveyance-two-messuages-two-gardens-and-two-orchards

> WILLIAM SHAKSPEARE. 95
>
> this little farm, the annual rent was eight pounds[2]; ⬅ which is above eleven shillings an acre, and near three times more than the usual rent of that time. Some peculiar circumstances attending the ground must have been the occasion of so high a price having been paid for it. <u>Probably there was a good dwell-ing-house and orchard upon it</u>[3]. ⬅
>
> In the short notes, which I have had occasion particularly to consider, the heralds mention that Mr.
>
> denture tripartite dated Dec. 11, 13 Eliz. [1570] and enrolled, between William Clopton and William Sheldon of the first part, Rice Griffin of the second part, and Edward Griffin of the third part, in consideration of 1550*l*. did fully and absolutely give, grant, bargain and sell to the said Rice Griffin all and singular the lands, tenements, &c. in Bishop Hampton, Stratford upon Avon, Ingon, the old towne of Stratford, &c. in the said former indenture par-

5

He 'Grew up in Town' Myth

Most people assume that William Shakespeare grew up in the town of Stratford upon Avon as this is what educators have always told us. Is there any written evidence to show where he was living? Let us jump to the year 1570. William Shakespeare would have been six years old and not yet in school.

> **Before a boy could be admitted into Stratford School it was necessary for him to have attained the age of seven, and to be able to read.**

Scholars tell us that John Shakespeare held several important town council positions. He acted as an alderman, an ale taster, a bailiff, and a council member. John even got elected as mayor in 1568.

Written proof exists that John Shakespeare owned a property on Henley Street, another on Greenhill Street, worked as a glover, and he baptized his children at the Holy Trinity Church. All of these things, scholars say, prove that John Shakespeare and his family lived in the city of Stratford upon Avon.

But this is not entirely true. John could have lived in the surrounding area just outside Stratford upon Avon **on a 14-acre farm** and done all these things too. Two sale conveyances in 1570 prove that John Shakespeare was occupying a 14-acre farm at that time. William Clopton sold a 500+acre property to buyer Rice Griffin. The sales contract stated: John Shakespeare has long been in the tenure or occupancy of 14 acres in Ingon Meadow. His lease started in 1564 and will expire in 1585.

The sale indenture states John Shakespeare was occuping 14 acres.

The description reads: "and also one other meadow with the appurtenances called or known by the name of Ingon, alias Ington Meadow, containing by estimation 14-acres be it more or less now or late in the tenure or occupation of John Shakespeare or his assigns."

Now, in the world of real estate, "his assigns" means "his transferee" so John had the right to sublease the property. At this, some people will jump up and down and claim, "It says John Shakespeare or his assigns, so John could have transferred the 14-acre property to someone else."

Yes, the document does say, "or his assigns", however, when a farm tenant DID sublease the property, Mr. Clopton made a note of it on his sale indenture. For example, Ralph Cawdrey was a farm tenant just like John Shakespeare and beside Ralph's name it says, "alias Cooke". The word "alias" means "otherwise called" Cooke and Mr. Cooke happened to be Cawdrey's son or son-in-law.

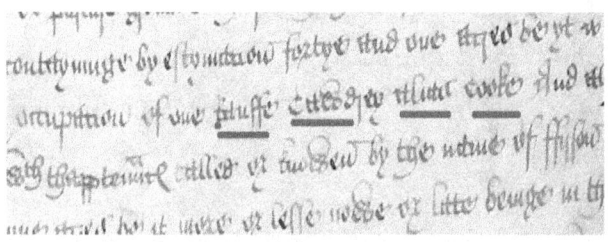

Ralph Cawdrey alias Cooke

Therefore, because there is not a John Shakespeare "alias Henry Shakespeare" or some other person after John's name, we cannot assume that John Shakespeare sublet or "assigned" his property to anyone. We have no written proof of it.

Backstory:

When William Clopton sold the property to Rice Griffin in 1570, he had to disclose all the various tenants to the new buyer. Clopton had plenty of money and built the house called New Place in the town of Stratford upon Avon, which was later purchased by William Shakespeare. (Note: Rice is also spelled as Ryce.)

Some Shakespeare-lovers disavow the sale indenture and will say, "This was just leased land. You cannot prove that a house was on *any* of William Clopton's property," but this is not true.

The word "messuage" means "house" and after the sale to Rice Griffin was finalized, the Queen "fined" William Clopton and his wife Ann for transferring two messuages with the 500 acres. Could there have been additional barns, outbuildings and dwellings with thatched roofs that were not considered messuages located on the 500 acres? Yes.

> Trin. 13 Elizabeth. Ryce Griffin, Esq., fined with William Clopton, and Ann, his wife, for 2 messuages, 500' land, 70 mead, 70' pasture, 200' wood, in Stratford, Ingon, Old Stratford, and Clopton, to him in tail, remainder to Edward his brother in tail, reversion to the right heirs of Edward Griffyn, his father.
>
> From "The Gentle Shakespeare"

Curious, I did a Google search for "Ington" Meadow, and what came up was a mention of "property once owned by *William Shakespeare's mother*".

Interesting too, John Shakespeare paid the highest rent of all William Clopton's farm tenants, yet others rented much larger parcels. So, might not this mean John and his family may have lived in a nice house in the countryside? Early Shakespeare scholars, like James

Halliway-Phillips, (1820-1889) believed so. Halliway-Phillips wrote:

"John (Shakespeare)'s rent was more than three times what others paid so it probably included a nice dwelling house with an orchard."

But wouldn't living on a farm interfere with John Shakespeare's town council meetings?

No, not at all. The meetings were brief and held only one day per month.

Other farm tenants like Ralph Cawdrey, Lewis Ap Williams, John Combe, and Richard Charnoff participated in town council meetings. They were elected to "important" positions. For example, like John Shakespeare, Ralph Cawdrey served as chief alderman too. William Clopton and Ralph Cawdrey also baptized their children at the Holy Trinity Church.

Lewis Ap William and Ralph Cawdrey owned property in town that they had leased out, which means John could have done the same thing too. So, did living on a farm a few miles from town stop these farm tenants from actively participating in their church and community? No.

Ralph Cawdrey

For Ralph Cawdrey (d.1588), yeoman of Stratford-upon-Avon, his will includes the following bequest:

To my son, William Cawdrey the younger, my house or tenement in Bridge Street in Stratford aforesaid wherein Mr Thomas Trussell now dwelleth.

Couldn't John Work as a Glover and Lease His Land to Someone Else?

Some folks ask why John Shakespeare could not have worked in town as a glover while subleasing his land to someone else. Do you think it is possible John might have done this? If so, keep in mind that records show that during the late 1560s and early 1570s, John Shakespeare worked as a "wool brogger". This means he would purchase wool illegally, then soak the wool in stale urine, and resell it to make a tidy profit. Where might John store this smelly wool? In his family's home on a 30-foot-wide lot in the city? Yech.

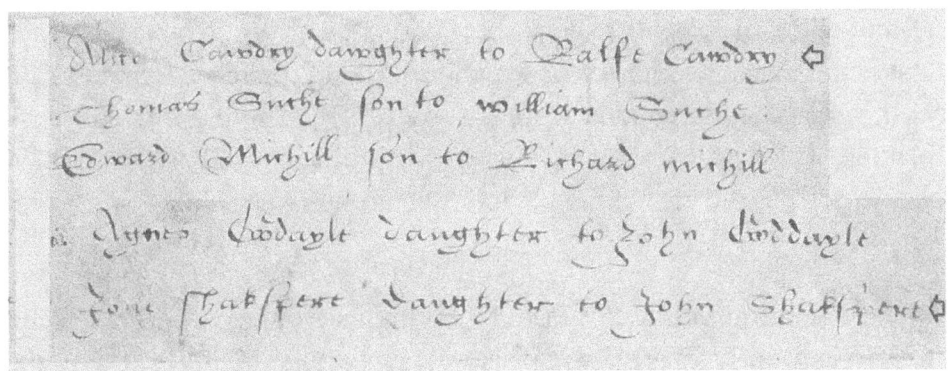

Ralph Cawdrey, farm tenant was the alderman when John Shakespeare was elected as chief alderman. They both baptized their daughters at the same church.

Plus, working on a farm is a 24/7 job. Sheep and cattle can be born on Christmas Day, and if they are left alone they can escape or predators might attack them.

Back in the late 1500s, selling wool without a license was illegal but those who did it made big money.

Dealing in large quantities of wool required horses or oxen, a cart, and a place like a barn to store the wool, treat it and deliver it. But from one sale alone, John Shakespeare managed to net £180 (worth $90,000 today.)

But working as a glover? Working men paid around 4d (pence) for a pair of work gloves, so John Shakespeare would have needed to make thousands of gloves to lend out £180.

He did call himself a glover when he appeared in front of a judge but referred to himself as a "yeoman" or farmer to everyone else. In a town with 25 glovers, a London judge might give him a more lenient sentence if he thought John Shakespeare was an impoverished glover.

Let us pretend that John Shakespeare sold weed, not wool, illegally back in 1571. Would a farm be better to grow it, or would a tiny 30-foot-wide lot close to a school be a good place? Might he need a barn to store his stash, and horses or oxen to cart the weed to customers? Yes. Well, John bought *two tons* of illegal wool in 1571 so did it make sense for John Shakespeare to live in town with this illegal wool? No. Back then people got paid for snitching so John would not want a neighbor to rat him out.

Living on a 14-acre farm a few miles from town offered John Shakespeare privacy. It would have helped his family survive the pandemic of 1564 too because during that year (the year of William's birth) one out of every three people died from the plague in the town of Stratford. John and his wife had lost two infant daughters to the disease while living in town so might his pregnant wife have wanted to move out for that reason alone?

Plus, a farm would provide milk, eggs, meat, and butter for his growing family.

Interestingly, John Shakespeare's 14-acre parcel was located next to 107 acres of farmland with a windmill. William Shakespeare purchased this same land from John Combe in 1602. Is this a coincidence? Or is it a clue, telling us that John Shakespeare may have lost the family farm, but his son bought it back for him.

Shakespeare-lovers, however, want people to ignore the fact that John called himself a yeoman or "farmer". But if there was a pandemic in town that was killing one third of the population, where would you want to live?

THE MYSTERY OF SHAKESPEARE'S LOST YEARS

Would you prefer to live in town with a lot of sick people? Or would you prefer to self-quarantine and keep your social distance by moving your family to a farm a few miles outside of town?

One Shakespeare-lover told me, "I would definitely live in town." When I asked, "Why?" She answered, "Because then I would be able to learn how to read. "Petty" schools were only found in towns and were not available for farm children."

What was a petty school? Back in the 1550s, most children learned their "A, B, C's" by attending the home of a local woman who would teach them. This was called a petty school. Grammar schools were different. For children to attend a grammar school (which taught Latin) there were two rules: Rule #1: he or she had to be seven years old, and Rule #2: he or she had *to already* know how to read.

Because John Shakespeare and his wife signed their names with a crude mark, it indicates that they were both illiterate. And, if John and his family lived on a farm outside of town, it makes it more difficult for William to have written the Shakespeare canon because there was no one to teach young William how to read.

Now do you see why knowing where Shakespeare grew up is important?

Living on a farm, William could have still attended school when he was older, and he may have learned how to read then. But Latin *was only* taught in grammar schools.

Finally, in 1602, William Shakespeare purchased 107 acres of farmland from John Combe. Who had John Combe bought this property from?

Rice Griffin, who had purchased it from William Clopton, remember them?

A Brief Recap

Living on a 14-acre farm a few miles from town offered John Shakespeare seclusion and privacy. It would have helped him to buy and sell wool as well as help his family survive the pandemic of 1564. More importantly, it would not interfere with his attendance at town meetings or going to the church that his landlord William Clopton attended. The question is, living on a farm, would William Shakespeare have learned how to read Latin at a grammar school? He might have learned Latin by teaching it to himself later in life, but is this likely?

Sources

The Plague in Stratford upon Avon: https://media.shakespeare.org.uk/documents/1564_The_Plague_Year_in_Stratford-upon-Avon.pdf

Nina Green's Translation: http://www.oxford-shakespeare.com/Chancery/C_54-843_mm_12-15.pdf

> investigation into the history of the ownership of the land in Old Stratford which William Shakespeare had bought from John Combe
>
> https://shakespearedocumented.folger.edu/resource/document/description/1542-deed-exchange-now-lost-lands-including-investigation-history
>
> ... exchange with Richard Catesby, had sold the land to Rice Griffin, that Rice Griffin had sold it to John Combe and that John Combe had ...

What Shakespeare Experts Say About His Education: https://www.shakespeare.org.uk/explore-shakespeare/podcasts/lets-talk-shakespeare/was-shakespeare-educated/

6

The Two Maidenheads Mystery

Was the property John Shakespeare bought in 1566 rented out? If so, how would we ever know today? In his book, *William Shakespeare: A Study of Facts and Problems*, author EK Chambers tells us that in 1582, John Shakespeare found himself involved in a lawsuit with a tenant named William Burbage for 7 pounds and 13 shillings.

Stratford upon Avon today

Chambers writes: "There was a dispute and an arbitration in London. (Burbage wanted out of his rental contract) and it was decided that John should repay Burbage £7 at a house called the Maidenhead."

Chambers continues: "Such payments were very often on neutral ground, and probably this assignation was not at John's *eastern* house later called the Maidenhead, but at another of which there is mention in 1597."

Remember how we had talked about how experts claimed John owned an Eastern and a western house?

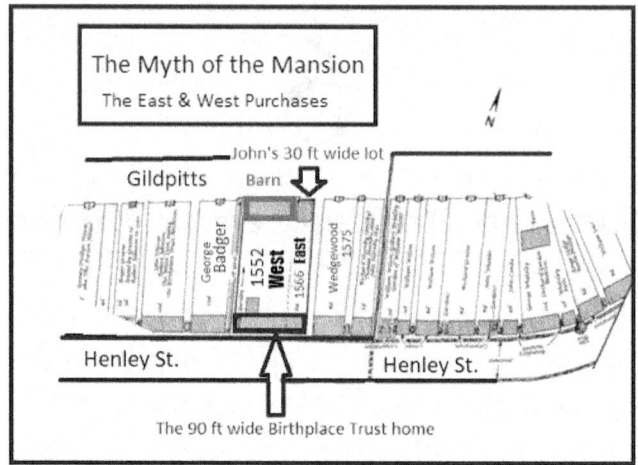

EK Chambers claimed there was "probably" another Maidenhead house mentioned in 1597, but I checked his source from 1597 and it mentioned only a barn belonging to John or William Shakespeare to the rear of the west property. It seems doubtful there was another house called the Maidenhead.

Chambers stated that the 1582 meeting preferably would NOT take place at any property owned by John Shakespeare, which makes a great deal of sense. Most likely Burbage would have preferred to encounter John at a neutral site. Preferably in public.

But think about it; both William Burbage and John Shakespeare *were in London* at the time they had agreed to meet. They had agreed to meet in Stratford upon Avon at the Maidenhead to settle their dispute. In a town with only 200 homes, would they really have been confused about where to go? No.

But why would Burbage visit a place known to be owned by John Shakespeare? Burbage would *never* do this because it might turn into a Christopher Marlowe-like-situation. The most well-known place in town called the Maidenhead was a tavern/inn that was built on the lot John Shakespeare had purchased in 1566.

Burbage must NOT have known that John Shakespeare owned it.

If in 1582, John Shakespeare and his family lived next door to Burbage in a tavern, why wouldn't Burbage assume John owned it? It makes more sense if John and his family were occupying a farm at Ingon Meadow. It would explain why people rarely saw John at the Maidenhead. John may have arranged it so that his tenant was responsible for paying the chief rent.

Most leases at that time were for long stretches, think ten years or more. But some commercial leases, like the one for the Maidenhead, ran for as long as 40 years. Interestingly, after John passed away in 1601, William Shakespeare handled the new lease for the Maidenhead and his language for this lease required the tenant, a man named Hiccox, to pay the 'chief rent'. Might he have learned this trick from his father?

My point is this: if the tenant paid the chief rent, how would the average person like William Burbage know that John Shakespeare owned the Maidenhead? He wouldn't.

If John Shakespeare (property owner) owed Burbage (tenant) money, either Burbage had been a tenant for several years, or he had just moved in. Either way, it does not seem like Burbage knew John Shakespeare owned the Maidenhead, located just steps from his rental house. The only reason we know that John did own the Maidenhead property is because he was still on record for paying the 'chief rent' of 6 pence.

Therefore, by all accounts, the place where Burbage was to meet John Shakespeare was the eastern part of the Birthplace Trust home, known as the 30-foot-wide lot on Henley Street first purchased by John Shakespeare in 1566.

But John Shakespeare never showed up.

According to Chambers, William Burbage had to sue John Shakespeare for recovery and the case dragged on for four years from 1588-92. Why did this lawsuit take so long? Like others before him, Burbage could not locate John Shakespeare. He could not find him in the town of Stratford upon Avon.

What has this to do with William's missing years? If John Shakespeare's farm lease started in 1564, the year William was born, then it means William was living on a farm until he got married in 1582. It also means that he and his five siblings were not growing up in the attic of a tavern.

Historical records show that not only William Burbage, but the Sheriff of Warwickshire and Henry Higford, the former steward for the Stratford Corporation in 1573 and 1578, could not locate John Shakespeare to serve him with a lawsuit. Back then, the forests outside of Stratford upon Avon were heavily wooded and dangerous, so most people would not venture into the area.

But nowadays, anyone with a computer and an internet connection can discover the whereabouts of William Shakespeare during the "lost years" of 1564 to 1582, because we can go online to the shakespearedocumented website. We can see the lawsuits filed by Henry Higford, as well as the actions from the sheriff.

I am going to repeat what I wrote in the previous chapter to emphasize that John Shakespeare was listed as a tenant of a 14-acre farm, located in Ingon Meadow in the parish of Hampton Lucy. (About 4 miles from Stratford upon Avon.) Type "Two Conveyances of Property in Warwickshire" into Google, and it will take you to the site where you can see the date: one hundred fifteen three scored and four = 1564.

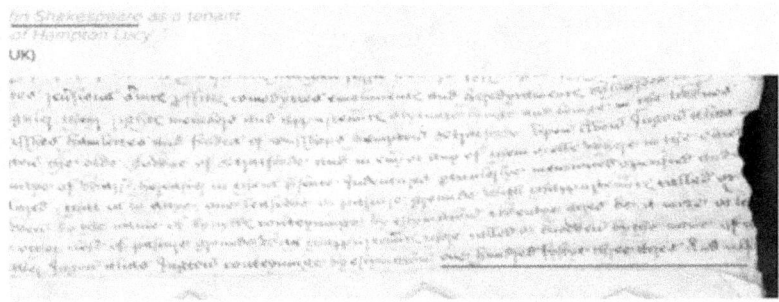

One hundred fifteen three scored & four = 1564

There appears to be two sale agreements: one for the land and the other for the tithes. Both were being sold at the same time from William Clopton to Rice (Ryce) Griffin.

Both contracts state that all the tenants' leases started on 1564 and ran for 21 years, so John Shakespeare's lease would have expired on or about April 30, 1585. What has this got to do with William Shakespeare's lost years?

A Brief Recap

If we are looking at these lost years as a "cold case" we must follow the evidence. Two contracts that were ratified by Queen Elizabeth in 1570 show that William's father were occupying a 14-acre farm in 1570 when William was six years old. The Shakespeare family did not live in town near the grammar school. Therefore, there is no proof William ever attended a grammar school and learned Latin.

Sources

Nina Green's translation:

http://www.oxford-shakespeare.com/Chancery/C_54-843_mm_12-15.pdf

7

A Mistake About Anne Hathaway

"Do you William, take this woman standing before you, to be your lawfully wedded wife?"

"I do."

With those words, William Shakespeare's life changed. Records show he and his wife were married in 1582.

Did you know that no evidence exists showing that his parents had attended his wedding? William was 18 and under the legal age of 21, so his father *should* have signed a marriage bond if he had approved of the nuptials, but John did not. Now, before we get into where William Shakespeare may have lived after 1582, the year he got married, a little backstory about Anne Hathaway is needed because most people are not aware of the mistake with her first name.

The Anne Hathaway Mistake

Most people are not aware Anne Hathaway's given name, the one her father called her by, was *Agnes* Hathaway not Anne. Feel free to fact check me by visiting the last will and testament of her father, Richard Hathaway on the Shakespeare documented website. There he refers only to Agnes, not Anne in his last will and testament.

According to Richard Hathaway's will, two of his trusted friends included Fulke Sandals and John Richardson, who were the guarantors of William Shakespeare's marriage bond.

THE MYSTERY OF SHAKESPEARE'S LOST YEARS

These two men would stand to lose 40 pounds if William Shakespeare's marriage to Agnes failed, or if it was later found there were any impediments as to why William should not have married her. One obstacle might have been the fact that Agnes was three months pregnant on their wedding day.

Richard Hathaway only mentions Agnes, my daughter - not Anne

Some researchers point to the fact that Agnes was almost eight years older than William Shakespeare. They slut-shame her by claiming she was 26 years old and desperate to have children. But this does not satisfactorily explain how Agnes and William got to know one another and became intimate. It sounds more like a bad joke where a traveling salesman spent the night in Richard Hathaway's barn, and schtooped the farmer's daughter.

My theory is that John Shakespeare had financial problems in 1578. A freak weather event may have caused severe flooding which could have wiped out his cattle and his crops. Insurance had not been invented yet.

So, if John Shakespeare was in dire need of cash as he had several mouths to feed, he may have outsourced William to work on the Hathaway farm. All the money 14-year-old William Shakespeare made by working as a laborer on the Hathaway farm would have belonged to his father John Shakespeare.

William Shakespeare probably continued to work on the Hathaway farm from age 14 to 18 and over the course of four years, Agnes and William got to know one another better. They became intimate as he was living there on the farm. He would have seen her daily at the Hathaway household.

For this reason, William would have gotten to personally know Fulke Sandals and John Richardson, and they him. As mentioned, these two men put up a substantial guarantee so they must have trusted that William and Agnes's relationship was solid. They put their money where their mouths were because they thought the union would stand the test of time. Does four years together seem like a normal amount of time for William Shakespeare to gradually woo Agnes and for her to fall in love with him? Yes.

The current theory claims that William Shakespeare had no time to visit Agnes. He lived in town and attended grammar school classes every day from 7:00 in the morning till 6:00 at night. He impregnated Agnes Hathaway without ever spending much time with her because she desperately wanted a baby. The two had a shotgun wedding and William's parents did not show up.

How does this relate to finding Shakespeare's lost years?

Agnes Hathaway could not read or write so she could not exchange letters with William. She could not text, email, or call him. Plus, she lived at a farm five miles away from Stratford upon Avon in a time when it took a man about two hours to walk five miles. So, if William truly did care for her, would he not need to spend time together with her? If he lived at her farm, he could have seen her often and others would have seen them too. This would have given them greater confidence to guarantee their marriage because they could see with their own two eyes that they were in love.

The Robert Peake portrait by DGA Brown Photography

In 1582, most women did not believe in having sex before marriage. Fornication was punishable by **'carting'**: being carried through the city in a cart, or riding backwards on a horse, wearing a placard describing the offence – an Elizabethan version of naming and shaming. So, if William had lived in town and wanted to see her often to woo her properly, it means he would have had to spend time with her. He would have had to visit her often. Would this leave him with much time for reading books and studying Latin?

The Years from 1582 to 1589

After getting married in 1582, William and Agnes Shakespeare could have lived either at John Shakespeare's farm at Ingon Meadow or Agnes's brother's farm in Shottery. The problem with living at Ingon Meadow is that if his parents had not attended the marriage ceremony, it might have been a bit awkward for Agnes to want to live there. In May of 1583, Agnes gave birth to their oldest daughter Susana.

Then, in 1585, William and Agnes welcomed twins: Hamnet and Judith.

Because his wife may have felt uncomfortable staying at his father's farm, William and Agnes and their three children most likely moved to Shottery to live on the farm Agnes's brother had inherited from her father, Richard Hathaway.

Records show that farm harvests were good during the early 1580s, so William would have been welcome to work there. Familiar with laboring in the area, the two men who had acted as sureties for his marriage bond, Fulke Sandals and John Richardson lived nearby, and worked as farmers. They all knew one another.

However, crop yields declined sharply in the late 1580s and early 1590s.

With a few years of bad harvests, William Shakespeare may have decided to leave for London to seek employment. This would have resulted in Anne staying in Shottery with their three children (and her brother).

The last will and testament of a shepherd named Thomas Wittington provides evidence that William and his wife must have stayed in Shottery. In Wittington's last will and testament dated March 25, 1601, he claimed that William's wife owed him 40 shillings or about £2 for watching sheep for Agnes (and William).

> Thomas Whittington, a shepherd living in Shottery, made his will on March 25,1601, signing by mark. He was buryied on April 19, 1601 and his will was proved ten days later. It included a bequest to "the poore people of Stratford" [of] XVs {40 shillings} that is in the hand of Anne Shaxpere wyffe unto Mr. Wyllyam Shaxpere is is due debt unto me being paid to mine executor by the said Wilyam Shaxpere or his assigns

Thomas Wittington kept long records of people who owed him money, no matter how long ago he had watched their sheep. And since he was asking for the money from the Shakespeare's to be given to the poor, he seems to be a trustworthy source.

By the way, in 1586, after John's Ingon meadow farm lease had expired, John Shakespeare's sheep and cattle had to go somewhere. So, perhaps John brought his flock of sheep over to the Hathaway farm where they would have been cared for by William and his wife. But when

William Shakespeare finally left for London, Agnes Shakespeare would have been stuck with them, so she hired Thomas Whittington to be her shepherd. The fact that a shepherd from Shottery claims William Shakespeare owed him money offers proof that William and Agnes must have been living in Shottery.

This now brings us to February of 1591 when it may have taken William five days to march to London seeking employment.

Coming from the farms of Warwickshire, William would have been good with horses and some people claim he may have found employment holding horses outside of theaters for wealthy patrons. There is no proof of this other than hearsay.

Or he may have looked up Richard Field, who worked as a printer in London, as John Shakespeare knew his father. (They were both leather workers.) This seems more likely.

However, as far as speaking in public or any stage acting goes, it seems far-fetched, mainly because of William's thick dialect. As the *YouTube* video shows, if Londoners today cannot comprehend what a Warwickshire man is saying, wouldn't it have been worse over 400+ years ago?

A Brief Recap

Richard Hathaway's two trusted friends put up £40 to guarantee that a marriage between William Shakespeare and Agnes Hathaway would last, even if Agnes was already pregnant. It seems unlikely they would put their money up if they viewed William as a book-smart city slicker who would quickly leave town after he had gotten a sweet local farm girl pregnant.

Sources

EK Chambers book:
https://archive.org/details/in.ernet.dli.2015.235169/page/n49/mode/2up

William's Marriage bond:
https://shakespearedocumented.folger.edu/resource/document/shakespeare-marriage-bond

Richard Hathaway's last will and testament: original copy

https://shakespearedocumented.folger.edu/resource/document/richard-hathaways-last-will-and-testament-original-copy

Edward de Vere

8

Was "Small Latin" a Big Mistake?

In 1623, Ben Jonson wrote that Shakespeare knew "small" Latin, which most people believe means William Shakespeare knew "little" or an "insignificant" amount of Latin. An "extensive" amount would be the opposite.

For this reason, Shakespeare-lovers argue that the "small Latin" phrase is taken out of context. They claim that Jonson had actually paid William Shakespeare a backhanded compliment. Taken into its entirety, Jonson's words meant William Shakespeare knew more Latin, or did not need to know Latin to excel beyond his contemporary playwrights as well as even the ancient ones.

This reminds me of a friend who used to go to bank meetings once a month. My friend attended these meetings for only fifteen minutes but was able to pay off his large mortgage debt in no time. He only looked anxious before his meetings when he would don his ski mask.

Similarly, I think it's a joke when people tell me that Shakespeare did not need to know much Latin to write *The Rape of Lucrece*. We will get to this later in this book.

Shakespeare-lovers argue that the "small Latin" phrase is taken out of context and that Jonson had actually paid William Shakespeare a backhanded compliment. One must read the entire verse that goes:

> And tell, how farre thou dist our Lily out-shine,
> Or sporting Kid or Marlowe's mighty line.
> And though thou hadst small Latine, and lesse Greeke,
> From thence to honour thee, I would not seeke
> For names; but call forth thund'ring schilus,
> Euripides, and Sophocles to us.

Taken into its entirety, Jonson sees William Shakespeare as an equal of the Greek and Roman writers Aristophanes, Terrence, and Plautus and of the Greek playwrights Sophocles and Euripides. Plus, he outshined his contemporary playwrights Marlowe, Lily, and Kid.

Shakespeare-lovers claim that knowing small Latin would have allowed Stratford to easily read a language like Spanish because it derives from Latin as do the other Romance languages: French, Italian, Portuguese, Romanian and Catalan. They reason that if someone knows Latin, they can figure out Spanish, French, and Italian too as they all evolved from Latin.

But does this ring true?

Some people will answer "Yes" but I disagree. I took Latin in school and speak Spanish fluently.

Latin may help one learn other Romantic languages, but to be able to read and comprehend entire books written in a foreign language takes time, even if one has a tutor and a great memory. Here is where Shakespeare-lovers will flash the "genius" card and claim that someone who is a genius could do this. He or she could pick up any language in a month or two.

Do you know a "small" amount of Spanish or French? If so, check out these verses from John Clapham's 264-line poem *Narcissus*.

Perque deos, multum promittere, fingere. Nullam
Quippe fidem regni nullamque Cupidinis olim   135
Dixerunt veteres, vereque haec comprobat aetas.
Muneribus tentes, quia multum munera possunt.
Quod castrum aut murus quis inexpugnabilis auro est?
Qualiscumque aliis, tibi semper amabilis esto,
Sisque tibi gratus, quoniam tu dignus amore,   140
Dignus amore tui, quem forma et mollior aetas,
Ingenium, vires, virtus, et cetera reddunt
Felicem; similem tibi tempora nulla tulerunt.
Sic tua te nimium lactabit opinio, donec
Umbra captus eris, caecusque peribis in illa."   145
Talia fatus Amor divellit ab arbore ramum,
Qui gelida maduit Lethaei fluminis unda,
Et teneri frontem, formosaque tempora spargens,
"Te posthac," inquit, "Narcisse, haud noveris ipse."
Hinc facie iuvenis mutari aut mente videtur.   150
Mox ascendit equum, qui caeca Libido vocatur,
(Quippe ferox numquam morsum neque frena ferebat)
Protinus ut dorso sessorem sentit inermem,
Cursitat huc illuc, iuvenis per devia fertur,
Per loca plena rubis, spinosa, incognita, dura,   155
Per iuga, per valles, puteos, latebrasque ferarum,
Per vada, per fluvios, per mille pericula, donec

It is not so easy to understand Latin, is it? You may be curious about the translation so I will provide it for you shortly. But first, next is a bit of the book *Precepts* written by William Cecil (aka Lord Burghley) and first published in 1616.

Beware thou spend not above
three of the 4 parts of thy re|venue,
nor above one third part
thereof in your house: for the
other two parts will but defray
extraordinaries, which will al|wayes

surmount your ordina|ries
by much: for otherwise
you shall live like Beggars in
continuall wants, and the nee|dy
man can never live happily,
nor contented, being broken
and distracted with worldly
cares: for then every least dis|aster
makes him ready to Mor|gage
or sell: and that Gentle|man
that sels an Acre of Land,
looseth an ounce of credit: for
*Gentilitie is nothing but ancient
Riches:* So that if the Founda|tion
do sinke, the Building must
needs consequently fall.

Precepts by Wm Cecil

The word "precepts" means "a general rule intended to regulate behavior or thought." A precept is a commandment or instruction. It is intended to influence someone else's way of thinking and it was all about being honorable. Below is the translation from *Narcissus*. Like *Precepts*, the author sounds like an old windbag as he offers instructions on how to behave. See for yourself. Compare Lord Burghley's advice in *Precepts* to *Narcissus* to see if you think the author is offering instructions to a young man on how he ought to deal with women.

> doesn't know what she wants. In her perverse way she won't want what you want. Now she wants, now she doesn't want. And now she hates what recently she had loved. So wandering a will is inborn into the female brain. Be eloquent of speech too, and wear soft clothing, varied in form and color. Remember to follow fashion: sing, dance, joke; at one moment play the lyre, at another write sad verses, in which, as is the fashion, you will lament fortune and fate; again, make vows; as proof of the sincerity of your words, swear by the stars and by the gods; promise much; pretend. For men of old have told how there is no honesty in government and none in Cupid; and truly this age proves the truth of this. (137) Assail her with gifts, for gifts can achieve a great deal. What camp or wall cannot be beaten down with a golden bribe? As you are to others, be always loveable in your own eyes, and be pleasing to yourself, since you are worthy of love, worthy of love of yourself—you whom beauty and soft youth, ability, strength, worth and everything else render happy. No times have produced anyone like you. Thus your opinion of yourself will allure you until you are caught by a shadow, and blindly perish in it." (146) So saying Love plucks a branch from a tree, which was steeped in the cold water of the river Lethe, and sprinkling it over the brow and fair temples of the tender youth, says, "Hereafter, Narcissus, you will not know yourself." From this moment the young man seems changed in appearance or mind. Soon he mounts a horse, which is called blind Lust because the fierce creature never endured bit or reins. (153) As

This chapter asked you to consider Ben Jonson's comment about "small Latin and less Greek." Was it a back-handed compliment? Or might Jonson have been warning future readers that the William

Shakespeare he personally knew lacked any sufficient knowledge of Latin?

Did William Shakespeare truly have the "means" the "motive" and "the opportunity" necessary to write the Shakespeare canon? If not Shakespeare, was there someone else who has been among us all along who could have written the canon?

It might be difficult for some people to know how to the answer this question, so, in this next chapter, we will look at things from the "devil's advocate" position and confront the Shakespeare authorship question head on. By this I mean, a growing number of people have signed a petition called "doubt about Will" that over the years has been growing and growing. It claims that Edward de Vere makes the most sense to be the "true" author of the Shakespeare canon. If this is true, here are some questions to consider.

If Edward de Vere *did* author the Shakespeare canon, why would he do so? What was in it for him? What would he get out of it – especially if William Shakespeare would get all the money and credit?

A Brief Recap

Some people mean well, but they talk too much. As the trusted advisor to Queen Elizabeth, Lord Burghley may have wanted the best for the young men under his care, but he may have come off as a bit of a windbag.

Links

The Shakespeare Authorship Coalition: https://doubtaboutwill.org/

9

The "Anyone Could Have Written the Plays" Error

There are some who argue that *anyone* could have written the plays of William Shakespeare. They claim all a person needed was a little imagination, empathy, research skills, discipline, and arduous work. But if this were true, why were Christopher Marlowe and Thomas Kyd mowed down in their prime? They both came from humble backgrounds, and both were successful playwrights. Marlowe has often been compared to Shakespeare in talent. However, the scholars who translated *Narcissus* believe Shakespeare wanted to "show his superiority". Why?

> Shakespeare may well have sought to establish the superiority of his own work. It may also have helped to create a nexus of associations between the myth of Adonis and that of Narcissus, which runs through Shakespeare's early verse.

The 800-pound gorilla people never talk about is Lord Burghley. Knowing that *Narcissus* was the first poem dedicated to Henry Wriothesley changes things. Especially when we learn the author of *Venus & Adonis* wrote a longer and better poem as an elegant response to *Narcissus*. So, the burning question is why? Who had a special relationship with Henry Wriothesley who *also* personally knew Lord Burghley?

The person *who intimately knew them both* must have written *Hamlet* too. Why *Hamlet*? In this play, the author mimics Lord Burghley's words of wisdom via the character of Polonius, who is depicted as being a boring, old windbag. Burghley's instructions for young men were put into a book called *Precepts* which was not published until the year 1616. Since Shakespeare died that year and *Hamlet* was performed around 1600, it is amazing that a lad from the Midlands would have known how to mimic Lord Burghley by having Polonius say:

> Give every man thy ear, but few thy voice:
> Take each man's censure, but reserve thy judgment.
> Costly thy habit as thy purse can buy,
> But not express'd in fancy; rich, not gaudy:
> For the apparel oft proclaims the man;
> And they in France of the best rank and station
> Are most select and generous chief in that.
> Neither a borrower nor a lender be:
> For loan oft loses both itself and friend;
> And borrowing dulls the edge of husbandry.
> This above all, – to thine own self be true;
> And it must follow, as the night the day,
> Thou canst not then be false to any man.

Does it not make sense that to make fun of him someone had to be personally close to Burghley? Burghley must have repeated these gems constantly. Interestingly, *Hamlet* was not performed until two years after Burghley's passing, most likely so to not anger his son, Robert Cecil who upon his father's death instantly became the next most powerful man in England.

The person most likely to write *Venus & Adonis* and *Hamlet* had to be Burghley's disgruntled son-in-law, Edward de Vere. Oxford had grown up in Lord Burghley's household and had lived with him from age 12 to 21.

But what about stylometry? Did not computer programmers prove Shakespeare's authorship? Stylometry counts the number of occurrences of certain words like "and" and "but". Some authors use them in a particular way that statisticians claim identifies them. The problem is *that not one letter* or journal or play known with 100% certainty to be written in the hand of William Shakespeare has ever been found. So, if the premise is to prove someone's identity, how can a computer scientist compare two samples of Shakespeare's writing if he or she only has only one published version? If the author Dr. Suess, for example, wrote during the Elizabethan era, might he write differently in a book than he would in his daily life?

So, let us look closer at Edward de Vere.

A Background Check of Oxford

Edward de Vere started learning Greek and Latin at the tender age of four. His childhood tutor was Sir Thomas Smith who had instructed college students in Greek at Cambridge College. He had worked as the court secretary for King Henry VIII.

Sir Thomas Smith owned an extensive library and believed it easier for someone to learn Greek first and then Latin. He and his wife were childless at that time, and they discovered young Oxford had a knack for learning.

Sir Thomas Smith

Having developed an extensive Latin knowledge early, Edward de

Vere attended classes at Cambridge College by the age of eight. He returned home at least four times a year to Hedingham Castle where his parents lived. His father owned a company of traveling players called The Oxford Men, so Oxford witnessed plays being written and performed at an early age. Did this inspire him to want to write plays?

Then at the age of twelve, Oxford's life changed forever. His father died and Oxford became a royal ward of Queen Elizabeth. He lived for nine years under the guardianship of Lord Burghley at Cecil House, an imposing mansion with a library ten-times bigger than his boyhood tutor's.

When Oxford was 13.5 years old, his tutor, Laurence Nowell, who was a mapmaker and dealer in rare books, including the epic poem *Beowulf*, claimed, "my work with the boy is no longer required."

Awarded honorary degrees from Cambridge College at age 14 and Oxford University at age 16, Edward de Vere also studied law at Grays Inn (a law school) at age 17.

Lord Burghley acted as Oxford's legal guardian and helped him avoid a murder charge at age 17 when an undercook died while Oxford was practicing fencing.

Later, Oxford married Burghley's eldest daughter, Anne Cecil, when he was twenty-one and she was 15, so Robert Cecil became his brother-in-law.

Oxford was admired by many who knew him as a great poet and supporter of the arts. Over 30 books were dedicated to him, but one of the most interesting links between Oxford's life and the writer of the Shakespeare canon is their mutual feeling of depression and melancholy.

A Brief Recap

The main point of this chapter: to familiarize the reader with our main suspect Edward de Vere aka Oxford. Back then, to attend a university, a student needed to pass a test providing he fluently understood Latin. At eight years old, Oxford passed the required Latin tests to attend college. In addition, Oxford had to take dance lessons every day, but back then there were no record players, CDS, or Spotify. So, would three musicians have to get up every morning before 7:00 am just so Oxford could practice his dancing? Most likely Oxford spent this time playing and practicing music himself as he was known for performing the lute.

But if Oxford is now our main suspect, why might he dedicate a poem claiming Henry was honorable? And if Henry was honorable, why would he visit Lord Burghley's house late at night to stop Henry Wriothesley from marrying his daughter?

Sources:

Edward de Vere short biography:
https://shakespeareoxfordfellowship.org/edward-de-vere/

Edward de Vere's music for the lute

Biography of Laurence Nowell:
https://www.wikitree.com/wiki/Nowell-682

Lord Burghley as Polonius

Alan H. Nelson

Oxford's Daily Regimine

7–7:30	Dancing
7:30–8	Breakfast
8–9	French
9–10	Latin
10–10:30	Writing and Drawing

Then Common Prayers, and so to Dinner

1–2	Cosmography
2–3	Latin
3–4	French
4–4:30	Exercises with his pen

Then Common Prayers, and so to Supper.

On Holy Days Oxford was to 'read before dinner the Epistle and Gospel in his own tongue, and in the other tongue after dinner. All the rest of the day to be spent in riding, shooting, dancing, walking, and other commendable exercises, saving the time for Prayer.' His tutor was Lawrence Nowell, Dean of Lichfield, brother of Alexander Nowell the scholarly Dean of St Paul's.[18]

10

The Queen's Mistake

For many years, writers compared Queen Elizabeth to a goddess. Edmund Spenser in the *Fairy Queen* referred to her as "Gloriana". Loyal citizens named her "Good Queen Bess" and because she never married, she was called "The Virgin Queen". Then came two works that were not so flattering: *Dido Queen of Carthage,* by Christopher Marlowe and *Venus & Adonis* by William Shakespeare. Both involved an older, powerful woman acting like a modern-day cougar. What if these two works hit Elizabeth too close to home?

Queen Elizabeth was known to have a nasty temper. Historian John Guy wrote, "She [Her Majesty] had a vicious temper, attacking one [of her handmaids] with her fists and breaking the girl's finger...Courtiers could bask in her sunshine, her favor, but they could also suffer her shouting, cursing and even violence. Only the foolhardy approached her if she was in a foul mood."

Queen Elizabeth was the daughter of Henry VIII who had two of his wives beheaded because they had failed to produce a male heir. The apple did not fall far from the tree.

What was the Queen's Mistake?

When Queen Elizabeth reached the age where she could no longer bear children, she told her friends she had entered a symbolic marriage with England as her husband. However, Elizabeth did have a special "friendship" with Robert Dudley, the first Earl of Leicester. She tried to keep this on the down-low, even though they were often seen holding hands in public. People were told they were childhood friends. This meant they could speak their minds freely and nothing improper would ever happen between them. Right?

Robert Dudley, the Earl of Leicester

Their closeness did not make Lord Burghley happy. He did not approve of the Queen's relationship with Leicester. Dudley was married, and if people saw the queen flirting with him or thought she was having an affair with him, they would have disapproved. Some might have jokingly called her 'Our Saucy Sovereign' behind her back.

What if Bess were to get pregnant? What would the Puritans say if Elizabeth got pregnant or had a child out of wedlock? Back then, an unwed queen having a son would be a scandal. Especially because the French duke of Anjou was seriously courting Queen Elizabeth. He wanted to make her his wife so he could unite the kingdom of France with England. Bess found him too young for her liking and frowned upon his Catholic faith. But she wanted to keep Spain at distance. They feared a French-Anglo alliance, so Elizabeth flirted with the French duke to keep Spain from attacking her homeland.

A Closer Look at the Dedication to *Venus & Adonis*

The dedication to *Venus & Adonis* reminds most people of someone of a low rank begging for a favor. Therefore, most academics claim that Edward de Vere, a high-ranking aristocrat would never write it. It would be "beneath" such a prominent earl to grovel like a commoner.

> To the Right Honorable Henrie Wriothesley, Earle of Southampton, and Baron of Titchfield.
>
> Right Honourable,
>
> I know not how I shall offend in dedicating my unpolisht lines to your Lordship, nor how the worlde will censure mee for choosing so strong a proppe to support so weake a burthen, onelye if your Honour seeme but pleased, I account my selfe highly praised, and vowe to take advantage of all idle houres, till I have honoured you with some graver labour. But if the first heire of my invention prove deformed, I shall be sorie it had so noble a god-father: and never hereafter eare so barren a land, for feare it yeeld me still so bad a harvest. I leave it to your Honourable survey, and your Honor to your hearts content which I wish may alwaies answere your owne wish, and the worlds hopefull expectation.
>
> Your Honors in all dutie, William Shakespeare.

The dedication to *Venus & Adonis* does sound like a commoner wrote it. But it makes sense for Edward de Vere to write it for two reasons.

One: No one would expect Oxford to "beg". No one. Especially Lord Burghley. He had witnessed an angry Edward de Vere challenge Phillip Sydney to a duel when the two were playing tennis. Sydney had just served when Edward de Vere arrived. He insisted that he ranked higher and demanded to use the court. Sydney refused, so Oxford challenged him to a duel. He claimed it was a matter "of honor". When Sydney walked away, Edward de Vere had famously called him a "puppy" or maybe it was a "pussy". You get the idea.

Two: The excessive "fawning" in the dedication may have allowed Oxford to sneak a coded message to Henry Wriothesley through dual meanings. I will explain why Oxford may have wished to communicate with Henry in a moment.

Might these words in the dedication hold a dual meaning?

- The first line reads: *I know not how I shall offend in dedicating my unpolished lines to your Lordship.* The word "unpolisht" suggests that the author considers his humble poetry to be unpolished or "unrefined."

- However, "unpolisht" can mean "straight-forward" and "direct" too. So, the writer might be saying, "I am dedicating my *sincere* or *honest* lines to you."

- The line, "*and vow to take advantage of all idle hours till I have honored you with some graver labor.*" Might there be a pun on the word "graver"? In Act I of the play, *The Taming of the Shrew*, the author wrote of "the grave citizens" of Pisa. Not until the late 1960s did someone discover a graveyard in the city of Pisa. The "grave" citizens were those in the cemetery!

  So, while most people think of graver as meaning "serious", it can mean "deadly" too. (As in, a labor that might cause the author to be put into a grave.)

- Another ambiguity arises in the line, "first heir of my invention". To most people, "the first heir" means the author is referring to the poem itself. For example, "This is the first product from my pen I have ever written." But this does not make sense because Shakespeare experts like Sir Stanley Wells claim that plays like *Henry VI* and *Titus Andronicus* were written well before *Venus & Adonis in 1593.*

- If the person who dedicated *Venus & Adonis* was Oxford, did the line about the "first heir" of my invention refer to his first use of the name William Shakespeare? Or was the author referring to Henry Wriothesley himself?

- If Henry was the author's first heir (i.e., the author's only male child) could not "of my invention" mean that Oxford loved him like Henry was his son?
- The next line "I shall be sorry it had so noble a godfather" does not refer to Henry Wriothesley as the godfather. The coded message indicates that Oxford might have been his godfather.

Let us suppose Oxford did not want Henry Wriothesley to marry his daughter and Lord Burghley was unaware of it. Why might Oxford be knocking on Lord Burghley's door late at night wanting to stop the marriage? The reason that makes most sense is this: if they married and consummated their marriage, Oxford's daughter, would have married her own brother. How would this happen if Oxford were only the godfather?

Hold that thought.

Pretend that Lord Burghley intercepted all communications from Oxford to the two lovebirds, what could Oxford do to stop the marriage? There was no phone, text, or email available. But what if he wrote a bestselling poem called *Venus and Adonis* and dedicated it to Henry Wriothesley? Dedicating it to Henry would set the record straight about his lack of honor, plus it might make him keen to read it. The message of not marrying Elizabeth would be subtle like how a wild boar kills Adonis. But Oxford knew how badly Lord Burghley wanted this marriage to succeed so he could not put his name on it. He would need to use an allonym to avoid the wrath of Lord Burghley. So, perhaps in 1592, Richard Field may have introduced Oxford to his penniless friend William Shakespeare.

But if Oxford was just Henry's godfather who was his mother?

"If the first heir of my invention prove deformed, I shall be sorry it had so noble a **godfather**, and never hereafter ear so barren a land, for fear it yield me still so bad a harvest."

The phrase "never hereafter eare" seems weird. What if the word "eare" is pronounced like "heir"? If so, when followed by "barren" seems odd because we normally talk of a woman being "barren" or unable to have children. It might be translated:

"Although you are not my son, then I am sorry because as your noble godfather I want you to know your (noble) mother never had a rightful heir, and we could never be a married couple." Who was the most famous "barren" noble woman in the world? Queen Elizabeth. Was she Henry's mother?

Could this be true? Certainly, Queen Elizabeth would not have wanted anyone to know she had given birth to a child out of wedlock. If so, there would be one hell of a lot of problems. Henry would be the rightful heir to the throne when she died. She would NOT be seen as "a virgin" and Catholic fanatics prodded by the Pope might wish to kill both.

Plus, what about her bargaining power with the duke of Anjou? If the duke knew Elizabeth was pregnant, would he still be keen to marry her? Might this cause Spain to attack England immediately?

The Earl of Oxford Bearing the Sword of State Before Queen Elizabeth at Windsor Castle on June 18, 1572.

Edward de Vere, born in 1550 was much younger than Queen

Elizabeth born 1533 and they were known to be close. She liked to dance with him and enjoyed his wit.

The View from 10,000 Feet Above Ground

Looking at this matter rationally, like sitting inside an airplane flying at 10,000 feet, is it possible Henry Wriothesley, born in 1573, was the secret son of Queen Elizabeth? If she did have a child out of wedlock, she would never acknowledge it. She did not believe in abortion so she would have allowed a wealthy family to raise him as their own.

According to many Oxfordian's (people who believe Edward de Vere wrote the Shakespeare canon). Yes. This secret holds the key to a better understanding of the plays, poems, and sonnets of Shakespeare.

Queen Elizabeth would not want the public to know that she had given birth to a bastard son. She wanted to keep up her reputation as the "Virgin Queen" and would do anything to silence anyone who knew about her "mistake". Wouldn't you agree she would NOT want people to know?

If so, you have just agreed with the term 'conspiracy theory' which simply means, "a secret of great importance that is being kept from the public."

Let us backpedal. If Henry Wriothesley was not Oxford's son and only his godfather, yet Oxford had read *Narcissus* where the author claimed Henry lacked honor might that ignite a godfather's temper?

Oxford was known for flying off the handle and being hot-headed. As a boy, he had challenged Phillip Sydney to a duel for not conceding the use of a tennis court to him.

Might Oxford fire off an 1,100+ line poem to defend his godson's honor? Yes. However, Oxford knew Lord Burghley was heartbroken over his eldest daughter's death, and Oxford may have been right to fear him. Burghley had always harbored deep suspicions that Oxford was solely responsible for her unhappiness, so Oxford wisely used an allonym to write *Venus & Adonis*. His name was William Shakespeare.

A Brief Recap

The idea of a bond between an individual and his society during the Elizabethan era involved a code of conduct that included various elements such as valor, chivalry, honesty, and compassion. Lumped together it was called "honor" and even though it was an abstract concept it still affected individuals. People would not rush out to the National Enquirer to blurt out intimate details to gain notoriety. Their sense of integrity or "honor" entailed keeping intimate details private out of respect for another person's reputation as well as that individual's feelings.

For this reason, an allonym was the "proper "vehicle to voice one's displeasure publicly, and poems with double meanings were written. But if you believe William Shakespeare of Stratford wrote the dedication and defended the honor of the youthful Henry Wriothesley, why did he suddenly change? Honor meant that someone had strict ideological principles that would never bend, but lending money and charging interest? That was not just "ungentlemanly". It was illegal.

For now, the years from 1593 to 1594 have been accounted for as William Shakespeare returned home to his brother-in-law's farm in Shottery to lie low with his wife and three children.

But *The Rape of Lucrece* offers another mystery. It has to do with WHY it was written and why someone was in such a hurry to publish it. And possibly who was the father of Henry Wriothesely.

Sources

<u>Venus and Adonis, first edition</u>

https://shakespearedocumented.folger.edu/resource/document/venus-and-adonis-first-edition

> **Chronology per Sir Stanley Wells**
> 3.1 *The Two Gentlemen of Verona* (1589–1591)
> 3.2 *The Taming of the Shrew* (1590–1591)
> 3.3 *Henry VI, Part 2* (1591)
> 3.4 *Henry VI, Part 3* (1591)
> 3.5 *Henry VI, Part 1* (1591–1592)
> 3.6 *Titus Andronicus* (1591–1592)
> 3.7 *Richard III* (1592–1593)
> 3.8 *Edward III* (1592–1593)
> 3.9 *The Comedy of Errors* (1594)
> 3.10 *Love's Labour's Lost* (1594–1595)
> 3.11 *Love's Labour's Won* (1595–1596)
> 3.12 *Richard II* (1595)
> 3.13 *Romeo and Juliet* (1595)
> 3.14 *A Midsummer Night's Dream* (1595)

In November of 1589, Queen Elizabeth "called-in" all copies of *Holinshed's Chronicles*. Yet scholars claim *Holinshed* was the source for Shakespeare's history plays. The 3 volumes were dedicated to Lord Burghley who would have kept copies of *Holinshed* at Cecil House.

https://www.jstor.org/stable/3817398

11

'The Rape of Lucrece' Mystery

Most mysteries will leave a trail of clues to follow. In this chapter we will have to follow the clues to figure out why *The Rape of Lucrece* (or just "*Lucrece*") was written and why it got to print in such a hurry.

Lucrece consists of 15,000-words based on seven books by two authors that had *never* been translated from Latin to English. Plus, it had to be approved by the Archbishop of Canterbury, John Whitgift, before it could be printed.

Most people today with a personal computer and an internet connection would have a tough time matching this feat. For example, what if Archbishop Whitgift took his sweet time to approve the poem?

Lucrece was anonymously registered in the Stationer's Register on May 15, 1594, or thirteen months after *Venus & Adonis* was published. Back then it took about *six months* for typesetting, and the source materials for *Lucrece* included seven books that had NEVER been translated from Latin to English.

Now, if you are a skeptic like me, you will be thinking, ha. There MUST have been some English translations available. I did look high and low but did not find any, but then again, I am admittedly lazy. What if the author had penned this poem prior to 1594?

It is possible, but back then, a person could make a name for himself by translating a book from Latin to English. Arthur Golding, for example, became famous for translating *The Metamorphoses* by Ovid in 1567. No one else had done it before him.

According to Carole E. Newlands, John Gower gained notoriety for translating the six books of *The Fasti* by Ovid in 1640. No one else had ever done it before him. Oh wait, except for one anonymous person. The author of *The Rape of Lucrece*. He must have done it prior to 1594 because Lucrece was based on the six books of *The Fasti*. This means the author of *The Rape of Lucrece* had to be an expert in Latin because these books by Ovid had never been translated.

> JOURNAL ARTICLE
> **The other John Gower and the first English translation of Ovid's "Fasti"**
> Carole E. Newlands

Plus, the other main source for Lucrece was *Ab Urbe Condita* by Livy. It is the *Founding of Rome* and came in 140 volumes with the first 30 books NOT translated into English until 1600. Feel free to do a search on your iPhone or Android.

The first book of *Ab Urbe Condita* runs about 650 pages, so we will only use Book One and the six books of *The Fasti* and call it a day. Imagine reading seven books all written in Latin that would have to be translated before *The Rape of Lucrece* could be written.

Face it, most of us would have a challenging time cutting and pasting John Clapham's 600-line poem *Narcissus* into Google Translate. Having to cut and paste the 650 pages of *Ab Urbe Condita* into Google Translate would make some students cry. We have become spoiled with things already done for us.

As mentioned, printing the poem involved the approval of the Archbishop of Canterbury and getting it back from him promptly was important. But would not someone with money get an approval faster than the Average Joe with no money? For example, if I'm flat broke and I requested that the Archbishop of Canterbury make it snappy, it seems doubtful that he would do so. But if I greased his palm with a few ~~hundred~~ thousand bucks? (Greedy bastard).

Finally, the "hard" publication date of May 15, 1594, must be honored because a clerk stamped *The Rape of Lucrece* in the Stationer's Registry on this date. The average page has about 500 words divided by 15,000 = 30 pages. I do not think that people today appreciate how difficult it would be to write a poem under this strict timeline using only a quill pen.

The Rape of Lucrece PROVES the "real" author was an expert in Latin.

May 15, 1594	Register at Stationer's
	Get the Approval by the Archbishop of Canterbury
	Approx 4-6 months of typesetting
	Write a brilliant 15,000 word poem in Iambic pentameter
	Translate 7 books from Latin to English that have NEVER been translated before.
April 10, 1593	I have an idea for a poem

If William Shakespeare wrote *Lucrece*, he had to write it earlier. Either that or be an expert in Latin who had access to many books. He would need money to bribe the archbishop too. But where would he find the books? There were no public libraries only private ones.

Lord Burghley's library did include *Ab Urbe Condita* by Livy. But William Shakespeare had no connection to him.

If Oxford, who had access to Livy, authored the poem, it still does not allow much time to translate *The Fasti* by Ovid never translated into English and draft the 15,000 words of Lucrece. But Oxford was 15 years older than Shakespeare, so he could have written it years ago and then revised it.

This still does not explain why it was written. And why it was penned so quickly? Nor does this tell us the identity of Henry's father.

A Brief Recap

Who was a known expert in Latin? Arthur Golding. He was credited for translating *The Metamorphosis* from Latin to English. Golding dedicated a Latin translation of the biography *Trogus Pompeius* to his nephew who he may have tutored. His dedication reads "to encourage you to proceed in learning." Golding dedicated the book to Edward de Vere and is dated 1564 which means Oxford was only 14 years old!

http://www.oxford-shakespeare.com/ShortTitleCat/STC_24290_Trogus_1564.pdf

---

The Latin in *Metamorphoses* Differs from the English Translation

The Latin in the original source, Ovid's *Metamorphosis* is "Rudis *indigestaque* moles".

The English translation is **"rude and pestered heap"**.

In *2 Henry VI*, 5.1.157 the hunchback Richard is addressed with: **"Hence, heap of wrath, foul *indigested* lump"**.

Metamorphoses consisted of 15 books and was first translated by Arthur Golding, the maternal uncle of Oxford.

The British Library claims Shakespeare read more than one version of *Metamorphoses*.

Two versions of *Metamorphoses* were at Cecil House because Golding lived there - so did Ed Vere.

12

The Lucrece Mystery Explained

Many mystery writers like to leave red herrings. Red herrings are false clues that lead us away from solving the whodunnit. They show us one thing while something else is going on at the same time. In our case, the historical records tell us Oxford returned home from a 15-month tour of Europe in 1576, and upon his return, he refused to speak to his wife for approximately five years. Why? Oxford claimed she was dishonorable. She had cheated on him.

Red Herring
Something meant to mislead or distract you

Nobody in history has ever believed him. Experts say that Edward de Vere treated his wife unfairly because Lord Burghley's daughter, Anne Cecil de Vere the Countess of Oxford, exuded class. She had no reason to be unfaithful. But Oxford? He was known to be eccentric and a first-class womanizer.

Edward de Vere could be physically violent one day and full of sorrow and remorse the next day. People were used to him throwing tantrums and Anne Cecil being a victim of his rage. But the question remains: did she cheat on him? If so, how would we know 400 years later?

Working the Math Backward

Let us suppose that a mystery man truly DID impregnate Queen Elizabeth and she DID give birth to a son named Henry Wriothesley. We know Henry's birthdate. He came into this world on **10/06/1573**. It is a fact. Now let us move backward in time.

Prior to this, Queen Elizabeth could have left London presumably to "avoid the plague." Therefore, quarantining in the country would allow her to wear pajamas and a bathrobe every day. Lazy people like me did the same thing during the 2020 pandemic. Might this help to conceal a pregnancy? It seems possible.

Going back even further means that Henry Wriothesley was conceived on or about **January 6, 1573**.

Ding! Ding! Ding! Does this date ring a bell? It should and not only with Proud Boy followers and Donald Trump.

Most Shakespeare-lovers in the house know that January 6th was also known as *Twelfth Night* a famous play written by William Shakespeare.

Interestingly, in this play, the main lead is a female character named Viola. Viola means *purple* in Italian. The royal color was purple. Only the Queen could wear it. The other main character's name was Duke Orsini and in Italian the word "Orso" means "bear."

Orsini means "little bear" which is interesting because Queen Elizabeth liked to give nicknames to people.

The Queen's nicknames included "Gloriana," the "Virgin Queen," and "Good Queen Bess" but in her closer friend circle, she called her lover, Robert Dudley, her "eyes".

Due to his short stature, she called Robert Cecil her "elf" and Lord Burghley her "spirit."

Her nickname for Edward de Vere was "Turk," possibly because he was fond of riding a horse named "ultra-marine" or Turquoise. Is it possible the name "bear" was a play on Oxford's last name? In Chicago, football fans are fond of "da bears". Did Elizabeth have too much to drink one night and call him, Edward "da bear" or even Edward da little bear?

Fast Forward one Year: 1574

Henry Wriothesley's first birthday happened on October 6, 1574, and a few months after this happy occasion, Edward de Vere left on his trip to Italy. If we go along with the theory of Oxford being the boy's godfather, he may have wanted to see his godson one more time before he left for Italy. It makes sense, right?

Oxford was leaving on a long and dangerous trip. There was no guarantee that he would come back alive to England to see his godson who he loved as if he was his own. The boy might one day be king.

The Facts of Record

- Henry Wriothesley was born on **10/06/1573**. One year later makes it 10/06/1574.
- Oxford's trip lasted fifteen months.
- So, if Edward de Vere left around Jan 1, 1575, then he should have returned to England around his birthday in April 1576.
- Historical records show that Oxford DID return to England around that time, and then had refused to see his wife.
- While away, Elizabeth Vere, Oxford's daughter was born on **07/02/1575**.
- But if we do the math backward, the conception date for Elizabeth Vere fell on or about the first birthday of Henry Wriothesley, **October 6, 1574**.

Wasn't this the time when Oxford was visiting his one-year-old godson, Henry Wriothesley?

So, after reviewing the math, does it make sense for Edward de Vere to believe that his wife had cheated on him?

Yes, but it is like the pot calling the kettle black. Oxford may have cheated on his wife with Queen Elizabeth, so perhaps his wife had yearned to get back at him.

However, this still does not explain the need to publish *The Rape of Lucrece* so quickly, does it? No. Nor does it explain the reason for the poem.

Unless, of course, Anne Cecil de Vere, Edward's wife had been raped.

Raped?

In the dedication to *Venus & Adonis* there was one word that jumped out at us. Remember? It was the word "honor."

> To the Right Honorable Henrie Wriothesley, Earle of Southampton, and Baron of Titchfield.
>
> Right Honourable,
>
> I know not how I shall offend in dedicating my unpolisht lines to your Lordship, nor how the worlde will censure mee for choosing so strong a proppe to support so weake a burthen, onelye if your Honour seeme but pleased, I account my selfe highly praised, and vowe to take advantage of all idle houres, till I have honoured you with some graver labour. But if the first heire of my invention prove deformed, I shall be sorie it had so noble a god-father: and never hereafter eare so barren a land, for feare it yeeld me still so bad a harvest, I leave it to your Honourable survey, and your Honor to your hearts content which I wish may alwaies answere your owne wish, and the worlds hopefull expectation.
>
> Your Honors in all dutie, William Shakespeare.

What about *The Rape of Lucrece*? Is there any word that jumps out? How about the word "rape"?

Raping a woman is not a subject that most people would author a lengthy poem about, but if we are saying that Edward de Vere wrote the Shakespeare canon, he must have had a reason. So, it must mean that his wife was raped. But who might be the rapist?

The first person to suspect might be the father of Henry Wriothesley. (We will call him the second earl of Southampton). He was in prison for 18 months and had few conjugal visits. Perhaps when he got out of prison and discovered that he and his wife "had been gifted with a son" that he decided to rape Anne de Vere. However, the second earl of Southampton was not only imprisoned in the tower of London at that time, but records show that he was seriously ill, so we can rule him out.

Who else?

What about Robert Dudley, the Earl of Leicester?

Three years into her reign, Queen Elizabeth desperately wanted to marry the Earl of Leicester, and it was rumored that Dudley was going to divorce his 28-year-old wife to make it happen. Elizabeth was so obsessed with Dudley that early in her reign she arranged for him to keep a bedchamber next to hers. This led to scandal and rumor. Many people, especially Lord Burghley, thought Elizabeth might be abandoning her country.

Lord Burghley believed Dudley was gaining too much power and influence.

Then on September 8, 1560, a tragedy happened. Dudley's wife, Amy Robsart, fell down a flight of stairs and perished.

Robert Dudley happened to be out of the country and could not be blamed for her 'misfortune,' but a coroner's report found two "dents" to the back of Amy's head that were half a thumb length deep and two thumb lengths long. Nails covered with pitch were found, so Amy's death was ruled a homicide. Who was responsible?

To this date, no one is certain. Like the mysterious death of Christopher Marlowe, some people think Lord Burghley may have been involved. Apparently, he was close to resigning before it happened. However, I am skeptical of this mainly because I am a fan of the true crime series TV show, *Dateline*. I have learned from experience that whenever a young, healthy female dies suddenly, the police immediately suspect the husband.

Robert Dudley had been seeing multiple women, but he had an airtight alibi. Knowing how badly he wanted to be king, he could have easily hired someone to kill his wife. Putting pitch around the nails in her head means she would not have bled much, and it would have seemed more like an accidental death.

After Amy's death, Queen Elizabeth suddenly got cold feet about marrying Dudley. The murder implication was not a good look. Still, Dudley did not give up on wooing the Queen. In 1575, for example, he lavishly entertained Queen Elizabeth at Kenilworth Castle.

But remember how Queen Elizabeth had made secret nicknames for people?

Her name for Robert Dudley was her "eyes," remember?

What is the one word that jumps out at us in *The Rape of Lucrece*?

The word **eyes**. It is used 42 times. If the poem was read aloud, the constant repetition of the word "eyes" might have made Queen Elizabeth squirm.

Suppose Robert Dudley (who died in 1588) had visited Oxford's house in 1574, and Oxford was not home. Would Anne Cecil de Vere have let Robert Dudley into her house? Yes.

When Queen Elizabeth was gone, Robert Dudley commonly acted like a "de facto" king. In those times, a king could have sex with any woman in England he desired. It was not a secret that a king believed he could rape with impunity.

How does this relate to the question of why *The Rape of Lucrece* was printed so quickly? Here are four possibilties.

Number One. You Killed the Wrong Guy. If playwrights Thomas Kyd and Christopher Marlowe were friends of Oxford, which they were, and they were all tortured and/or killed because Burghley assumed Shakespeare was the allonym of Marlowe, why not publish Lucrece on the one-year anniversary of Marlowe's death? Might publishing it on May 30 help commemorate Marlowe's life? Yes, and if not, it would drive Burghley crazy knowing that the "real" author was still out there.

Number Two. It Explains who *was* Guilty. If Lord Burghley was constantly berating Oxford or faulting him for his daughter's unhappiness, then perhaps *Lucrece* was an opportunity to explain to Burghley the truth of why his daughter was always so unhappy.

The Rape of Lucrece explains it was not ALL Edward de Vere's fault. Robert Dudley, the real monster was to blame for ruining the lives of both Anne Cecil and Oxford. But Dudley had died in 1588 so nothing could be done to him.

Number Three. To Stop Future Killings. In *The Rape of Lucrece*, the plot goes like this: after Tarquin had raped Lucretia, he told her that he was going to tell her husband that he had caught her having sex with a slave. Who would her husband believe? It would be Tarquin's word against Lucretia's. What could Lucretia do? Nothing. Right?

Not true. Lucretia sent a secret message to her husband and her father to meet at her house. Tarquin came too. In front of all three men,

Lucretia confessed. She told her father and husband that Tarquin had raped her. Saying that she could not live with herself, Lucretia stabbed her stomach with a knife. *The Rape of Lucrece* ends with her suicide. Therefore, what if Edward de Vere had threatened to commit suicide? Doing so would ruin the lives of Lord Burghley's three granddaughters. But Oxford did not seem afraid of taking his own life.

Number Four. I know the truth. Looking like a dead-ringer for actress Cate Blanchett in a long, flowing dress, Queen Elizabeth tells Lord Burghley not to leave the room. She then tells Oxford: "I believe your wife. She claims she was raped by Robert Dudley. Well, **I was also raped by Robert Dudley. He is the father of Henry Wriothesley, not you, but of course, you knew this.** How do I know? Because a little bear can be found on Robert Dudley's coat of arms, and in *Twefth Night* you named the character **Duke Orsini**. Although I was raped, I gave the child up for adoption, and pretended to show affection towards Robert Dudley. As a result, he died never knowing of his son's royal birth. For this reason, you were wise not to allow your daughter Elizabeth Vere to marry Henry Wriothesley, or she really would have married her own brother." Edward de Vere nods. "Therefore, I, Queen Elizabeth promise *not* to kill you and/or your allonym (William Shakespeare) as long as you vow to keep my secret safe. History must never know that I was raped."

Now, if this was true, how would we know Queen Elizabeth kept her word that neither he nor his allonym would be harmed in the future? One clue is after the publication of Lucrece, in 1594, the name William Shakespeare showed up in the Queen's pay list. Guess who picked up his money and was free to walk about the streets of London unharmed and never questioned by Lord Burghley? William Shakespeare.

In 1601, Queen Elizabeth's reaction in the Essex Rebellion shows that she knew who the real author was, and never harmed the Stratford man. We will talk about the Essex Rebellion later, but first, ever hear of "Boxing Day"? It is a British holiday celebrated after Christmas Day that occurs on the first weekday after Christmas.

A boxing day mystery involves William Shakespeare.

A Brief Recap

People ask me if I read through every single play and count words, but as you already know, I am far too lazy for that. How lazy am I? I admire the person who created the Japanese flag. So, if you are lazy like me, a cool website to check out is www.shakespeareswords.com. You can add a word to the search field (like "eyes"), and it will count the number of times it is found for you. By the way, this idea that Queen Elizabeth was raped is my own personal observation, and has not been accepted by any mainstream scholars.

Sources

Podcast: Don't Quill the Messenger: https://shakespeareoxfordfellowship.org/

Rebecca Larson: https://tudorsdynasty.com/the-unvirgin-queen/

https://www.google.com/books/edition/A_Collection_of_State_Papers_Relating_to/OXBXAAAAcAAJ?hl=en&gbpv=1&bsq=1573

Ab Urbe Condita first translated by Philemon Holland in 1600 http://www.perseus.tufts.edu/hopper/text?doc=Perseus:text:1999.02.0151

Robert Dudley's Coat of Arms feature a little bear

13

The Boxing Day 'Mistake'

Some mysteries feature exotic detectives like Hercule Poirot, but I am assuming that you are an Average Joe like me. If you're like me, you are probably great at helping to find things around the house. In fact, I often like to help by pointing out that "it's got to be around here somewhere."

When we last left our caper, *Lucrece* was registered. The theaters, which had been closed to the public due to the plague, reopened and people came out in droves to see plays. Kind of like people viewing the movie *Top Gun Maverick* after the worldwide COVID pandemic.

Due to pent-up demand, from June of 1594 to December of 1594, the Lord Chamberlains Men, of which William Shakespeare was a member, performed every other day. (This is according to the Encyclopedia Britannica).

Even during the final week of December 1594, The Lord Chamberlain's Men played before Queen Elizabeth twice. Once on Saint Stephens Day (December 26th) and the other happened on Innocent's Day (December 28th).

Why is this important? The Lord Chamberlain's Men received £24 for these two unnamed performances and William Shakespeare's name shows up on the Queen's paylist. He is someone eligible to collect the payment. Experts claim this proves beyond a shadow of a doubt that William Shakespeare was an actor who had acted in two unnamed plays before Queen Elizabeth on that last week of December 1594.

Here is the problem.

THE MYSTERY OF SHAKESPEARE'S LOST YEARS

An Article by Holger Schott Syme tells us, *A Comedy of Errors* was staged on 28 December 1594, (Innocent's Day) during the Christmas revels at Gray's Inn (a law school).

A second account from the Gesta Grayorum confirms this. It claims that *The Comedy of Errors* was first staged on 28 December 1594, during the Christmas revels at Gray's Inn. This article claims "it was **played by the Players**". This means these players wished to remain anonymous.

> good not to offer any thing of Account, saving Dancing and Revelling with Gentlewomen; and after such Sports, a Comedy of Errors (like to *Plautus* his *Menechmus*) was played by the Players. So that Night was begun, and continued to the end, in nothing but Confusion and Errors; whereupon, it was ever afterwards called, *The Night of Errors*.

So, what is the big deal?

The rule was that Queen Elizabeth got to see all the new plays first. Remember how the account from Gesta Grayorum claimed the players at Gray's Inn were *anonymous*?

The Lord Chamberlains Men were NOT a group of unknowns. They would have been recognized and named as the players. So, modern Shakespeare experts claim a mistake must have been made by someone. No big deal. But two published versions said the play happened at Gray's Inn on the 28th. Let's say it was a mistake and Errors played before the Queen on the 27th. If so, then the historical payment record must be wrong too because it shows only the dates of St. Stephen's Day and Innocents' Day.

1595-3-15: **Royal record.** An entry in the accounts of the Treasurer of the Chamber reads: "To William Kempe, William Shakespeare and Richard Burbage, servaunts to the Lord Chamberleyne, upon the Councille's warrant dated at Whitehall XVth Marcij 1594, for two severall comedies or enterludes shewed by them before her majestie in Christmas tyme laste part viz St. Stephen's daye and Innocents daye..." (Public Record Office, Pipe Office, Declared Accounts No. 542, f. 207b).

The Comedy of Errors sparkles with metaphors and puns about the law. Performed by "anonymous" players for free in front of law students at Gray's Inn, it caused a stir from the dignitaries and important people because one account claimed there were 'gentlewomen whose sex did privilege them from violence.'

Edward de Vere had attended the Gray's Inn law school. He knew what it felt like to be all alone studying law during the Christmas holidays. He knew most of the actors called The Admiral's Men who featured his friends, Will Kempe and Edward Allyn. Might they have performed the play that night for their pal Oxford while the Lord Chamberlain's Men received payment for performing before the Queen? It seems possible.

Also, if the Queen had already seen *The Comedy of Errors* previously then it could have been performed at Gray's Inn without issue while The Lord Chamberlains Men were performing before the Queen. The problem is that an earlier performance date before the Queen would not fit the narrative of a boy genius, so Shakespeare experts blame a clerk. They say someone "must have" made a mistake.

Let us think logically about this: historical records show that *The Rape of Lucrece* was rushed to the press in May of 1594. Then William Shakespeare's company of players performed almost every night after June of 1594. Finally, opening night for *The Comedy of Errors* happened on December 28, 1594.

Wouldn't the anonymous players performing *The Comedy of Errors* need a copy of the play in advance to rehearse their lines before opening night?

Could William Shakespeare have been able to pull off jotting down a play about the law without studying it? Would he have time to study the law and write the play for a group of anonymous players to perform it in time for what happened at Gray's Inn on December 28?

Things make more sense if *The Comedy of Errors* **was older** than 1594. This way the group of anonymous players, would have had plenty of time to learn their lines and rehearse the play. They would not just show up and expect to wing it somehow.

An article called *Portals of Discovery* by A. Bronson Feldman explains the history of *The Comedy of Errors* in greater depth. Feldman claims in 1577, the singing children of St. Paul's Cathedral had acted a play before Queen Elizabeth and her court named "*The History of Error.*" (See the article under Sources).

Since we have already talked about the years 1593 to 1594, when *Venus & Adonis* and *The Rape of Lucrece* were written, let us now jump backwards in time to 1592.

A Brief Recap

Common sense tells us that *The Comedy of Errors* must have been written well before it's performance in 1594, but Shakespeare-lovers refuse to admit to it.

Sources

A History of The Comedy of Errors can be found in *Portals of Discovery* by A. Bronson Feldman:
https://www.jstor.org/stable/26301648

On New Year's night 1577 the singing children of St. Paul's Cathedral, under the direction of Master Sebastian Westcott, acted a play for Queen Elizabeth and her court, named in the accounts of the royal Office of the Revels "The History of Error".[1] Nothing is known about the plot of this drama, but a number of experts on the Tudor theater have guessed from its odd title that it was an early version—if not the protoplast—of Shakespeace's *Comedy of Errors*. The

14

The Clayton Loan Mystery

In 1592, the year before the publication of *Venus & Adonis*, an unknown actor named William Shakespeare came into some unexpected money. We know this stroke of good fortune happened in 1592 because eight years later, William "Shackspere" sued over it. The lawsuit in 1600 claimed William Shakespeare had lent £7 to John Clayton, a yeoman from Willington, Bedforshire.

In his complaint, filed in London, William Shakespeare requested a total of £10 which included a £3 penalty. He claimed he had lent John Clayton the money in 1592 but had never been repaid. The judge ruled in William Shakespeare's favor and so it places William Shakespeare in London in 1592 with plenty of money in his pocket. Or does it?

Most Shakespeare-lovers disagree. Like Obi wan Kenobi they will claim, "This is not the William Shakespeare you are looking for." Why? They claim this man spelled his name differently and he "could have" hailed from Campton, Bedfordshire (about eight miles from where John Clayton lived in Willington, Bedfordshire). They say "could have" hailed from because no one is sure. It is a mystery.

An amateur sleuth named John Rollet researched things. He wondered who had acted as William Shakespeare's attorney for this court case. The answer: Thomas Awdley, who was a citizen and grocer of London. Digging deeper, Awdley's father hailed from Willington, Bedfordshire so Rollet concluded that the William Shakespeare who had lent the money had to be from Willington, Bedfordshire too. Case closed, right?

William Shakespeare had lodged his complaint in London. This means that the transaction must have taken place in London. Therefore, why would someone from Bedfordshire travel 55 miles for £7?

It's not like it was for £700 or £7,000 it was only £7. If they both knew each other and were from Bedfordshire, why not meet there?

So, the question remains: were the two men from Bedfordshire, or had William Shakespeare of Stratford upon Avon come into some money while in London and had lent someone a small amount?

Digging even deeper it turns out that Thomas Awdley, the citizen, and grocer of London who had acted as Shakespeare's attorney DID have a connection to Stratford upon Avon. Thomas Awdley appointed Mr. Thomas Greene, from Stratford upon Avon, to be the overseer of Awdley's last will and testament.

So, Thomas Awdley, William's attorney in London did have a connection to Stratford upon Avon. If not, why would he hire Thomas Greene to oversee his own last will and testament? If Thomas Awdley were from Willington, why not hire an attorney from Willington?

For this reason, it appears our boy William Shakespeare had lent the £7. He was fond of taking people to court for lesser amounts of money and scholars claim he had left Stratford upon Avon for London to find work around 1591. The question is, where did William Shakespeare suddenly find the cash in 1592 to lend out so freely?

The last we had heard of him; William Shakespeare did not have a pot to pee in. Flat broke, he had kissed his wife and three children goodbye and had hoofed it to London seeking employment.

Was a rich earl named Edward de Vere willing to pay a handsome amount of money to someone to use his name to defend Henry Wriothesley's honor? Was William Shakespeare the allonym for Edward de Vere?

A Brief Recap

We know William Shakespeare went to London because there was a letter written to him there, and entries in the British National Archives show that he regularly failed to pay his taxes. But when confronted with the loan to John Clayton in 1592, Shakespeare-lovers will sound like Obi-Wan-Kanobe and say, "This is not the William Shakespeare you are looking for." Why? The loan to John Clayton in 1592 proves William Shakespeare suddenly came into some unexpected money that cannot be explained.

Sources

https://shakespeareoxfordfellowship.org/wp-content/uploads/ER1996-v4-1A-Price_Shake-Clayton-Loan.pdf

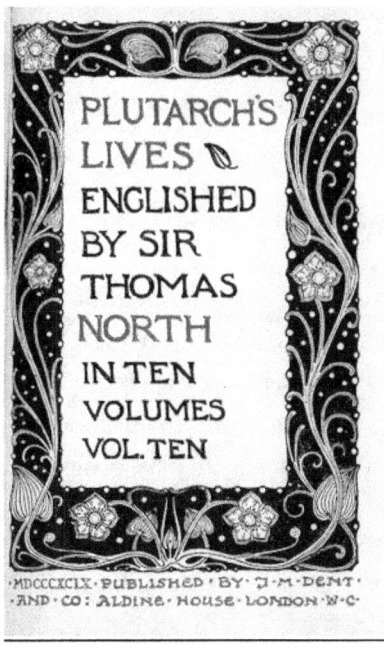

15

The Myth of Oxford's Bad Poetry

Most good mysteries involve a surprising twist or two. In our case, experts say Oxford wrote god-awful poetry. Here is a prime example of it called *Loss of My Good Name*.

> Framed in the front of forlorn hope, past all recovery,
> I stayless stand to abide the shock of shame and infamy.
> My life through lingering long is lodged,
> in lair of loathsome ways,
> My death delayed to keep from life,
> the harm of hapless days;
> My spirits, my heart, my wit, and force,
> in deep distress are drowned,
> The only loss of my good name,
> is of these griefs the ground.

Oxford's Poetry

If the poem *Loss of My Good Name* does not float your boat and/or seems like a lame poem written by a seventh grader, it might be because this poem WAS written when Edward de Vere was only 14 to 16 years old. He loved classical allusions in his poetry like referring to Hannibal the general who had attacked Italy by crossing the Alps.

Loss of my Good Name was found in an anthology first collected by the Master of the Children of the Chapel Royal, Richard Edwards who had assembled several of his favorite songs or poems with the intent of publishing them. But Edwards died unexpectedly in 1566, so the collection sat on a shelf and went unpublished for about ten years.

The Paradyse of Dainty Devices was eventually published in 1576 and was found in the collection of Sir John Hawkins who was the historian of music. This has led many people to believe Edwards' collection of "poems" were most likely songs.

Loss of my Good Name offers a good example of Oxford's poetry. It has tragic melancholy sprinkled with alliteration throughout it like "stayless stand," "lingering long" and "death delayed." If we were looking for a criminal who used tragic melancholy and alliteration throughout his works, then Oxford's poems fit the bill.

But ever notice that many modern songs feature alliteration in them? *Drops of Jupiter* by Train has "And are you lonely, looking for yourself out there?" What about *Lovely Rita* by the Beatles? "Made her look a little like a military man." Or *Mean Mister Mustard* also by the Beatles, "Mean mister mustard sleeps in the park". Don't forget, the chairman of the Board himself, Frank Sinatra sings in his song, *That's Life,* "I've been a puppet, a pauper, a pirate, a poet, a pawn, and a king." Even more recently, in the song *Kill You* Eminem raps "I invented violence, you vile, venomous, volatile and vain, Vicodin, vrinn, vrinn." Perhaps the use of alliteration might make it easier for a singer to remember the words to sing.

Now, people today might think Edward de Vere's poems in *The Paradise of Dainty Devices* are god-awful bad, but the book got reprinted *ten* times. So, to most of our ancestors, the book was a hit! Elizabethans loved it.

Looking closer, another song called *"Where Griping Grief the Heart would Wound"* matches Edward de Vere's tragic, melancholic lyrics filled with alliteration. We hear it in the words "Griping grief," "doleful dumps" and "silver sound." It is also found in *The Paradise of Dainty Devices.*

So, if this is a mystery, where is the surprising twist?

How does this relate to William Shakespeare's lost years? Well, the words "griping grief," "doleful dumps", and "silver sound" are found in Act 4 Scene 5 of the play *Romeo & Juliet* allegedly written by William Shakespeare.

Type the phrase "When griping grief, the heart doth wound" into the *YouTube* search engine and it will open a video to musicians playing this song. A search on Google images shows that the lyrics have musical notations, but it does not say Edward de Vere wrote it. The song is attributed to Richard Edwards. To this day the poem is found in *music* books.

When Griping Grief The Heart Doth Wound

Did you know Edward de Vere owned a lute and played in recitals at Whitehall Castle? It is true. In addition to his songs, he had written a play when he was almost 16 that was such a hit that it was mentioned in a book twenty-three years later: even though it may have only been performed a few times.

Richard Edwards died in 1566 but incredibly, twenty-three years after his death, George Puttenham credited Richard Edwards and Edward de Vere in *The Arte of English Poesie* for writing two plays: one a comedy and one an interlude. They had to be written before Oxford had turned 17 years old as Oxford was born in 1550 and Richard Edwards died in 1566.

But if Edward de Vere wrote poems when he was older, might his writing style have changed? Are the poems you wrote when you were 16 the same as your poems today?

If Edward de Vere wrote melancholy song lyrics at age 16, might he write melancholy sonnets at age 40?

> Th'Earle of Oxford and Maister *Edwardes* of her Majesties Chappell for Comedy and Enterlude. For Eglogue and pastorall Poesie. Sir *Philip Sydney* and Maister *Challenner*, and that other Gentleman who wrate the late shepheardes Callender. For dittie and amourous *Ode*
>
> –George Puttenham "The Arte of English Poesie" of 1589

Here is another surprising twist; in 2006, a British physician, Dr. Ken Heaton, drafted a paper called: *"Faints, fits, and fatalities in Shakespeare."*

Dr. Heaton, a medical doctor, noticed how ten deaths from 'strong emotion' occurred in the playwrights late works, as well as 'transient loss of consciousness staged or reported' found in 18 works, and 13 episodes of 'near-fainting'.

This raises the question: why all the swooning and near-fainting in Shakespeare? Why did so many works of Shakespeare feature this syndrome while the works of other contemporary artists did not? It must be something unique to the writer.

To state the obvious: the real author of the Shakespeare canon must have been familiar with fainting. Today most of us would associate fainting with epilepsy, which may be correct, but it might be wrong too. There can be other reasons why a person faints. Hold that thought.

Fast forward to the pandemic year of 2020. One morning while watching daytime TV (a luxury I enjoyed during the epidemic) I could not help but notice the many commercials for "Latuda." It made me wonder how much "Latuda" cost and what problem did this drug solve for regular daytime TV-watchers? Certainly, these commercials were not free or inexpensive.

I learned Latuda cost $1,500 for a 30-day supply, and the drug treats bipolar disorder. What is bipolar disorder?

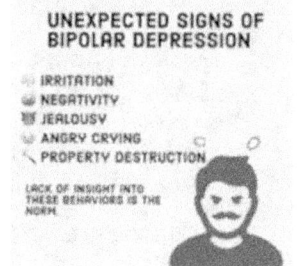

Formerly called manic depression, bipolar disorder (or BD) is a mental health condition that causes extreme mood swings. The side effects of Latuda the announcer mentioned included "fainting." His words went something like: "You may feel lightheaded or faint. Latuda may make you sleepy or dizzy which may lead to falls that can cause fractures or other injuries, seizures, or convulsions."

So, to clarify, the medication may induce fainting. However, when I did a Google search about fainting and bipolar disorder, I learned that "syncope (fainting) is common in psychiatric disorders" which means if people are fainting regularly, it is not uncommon for them to have a psychiatric disorder like bipolar disorder.

Later that same day, I was doom-scrolling on Twitter and watched a video of Sir Patrick Stewart reading a Shakespeare sonnet. Patrick sounded so filled with woe and despair, that I joked aloud, "Wow. It sounds like old Shakey could have used some Latuda." Then I realized, Holy Cow. What if this were true? What if the real author of Shakespeare was bipolar?

Obviously, back in the sixteenth century, people did not understand what caused manic depression. They thought someone was possessed by a demon so they would beat them with a stick. (Hence the expression "beat the devil out of you.") Also, back then, most people associated fainting with epilepsy. But the more I thought about it, the highs and lows described in the Shakespeare canon resembled bipolar disorder symptoms more than epilepsy. However, the term "bipolar disorder" did not become a label until 1980.

Some medical professionals today theorize that childhood epilepsy can morph into bipolar disorder when a child reaches their early 20s.

If the "real" author of the Shakespeare canon had endured bipolar disorder, might he have found an escape in music? Did music help to relieve stress and comfort him after losing his parents? After all, many bipolar musicians have told us similar tales. Modern musicians enduring BD include:

- Scott Stapp, the lead singer for Creed and Art of Anarchy.
- Mariah Carey
- Halsey
- Sia
- Pete Wentz of Fall Out Boy
- Selena Gomez
- Bebe Rexha
- Adam Ant
- Demi Lovato
- Ray Davies of the Kinks
- Kanye West

Now, what if, the "real" author had written plays, poems, and sonnets to reveal his feelings of living with this mysterious illness? Might this explain why Shakespeare was so prolific?

Did you know that writer and actor Carrie Fisher, featured as Princess Leia in *Star Wars,* lived her whole life with bipolar disorder? It is true. She once wrote: "You know how most illnesses have symptoms you can recognize? Like fever, upset stomach, chills, whatever. Well with bipolar disorder it's *sexual promiscuity, excessive spending, and substance abuse* – and that just sounds like a fantastic weekend in Vegas to me!"

According to the Mayo Clinic, manic symptoms of BD include:

- Abnormally upbeat, jumpy, or wired
- Increased activity, energy, or ***agitation***
- Exaggerated sense of well-being and self-confidence (euphoria)
- Decreased need for sleep.
- Unusual talkativeness
- Racing thoughts – feeling anxious, light-headed, and *sometimes fainting*
- Distractibility
- Poor decision-making — for example, going on buying sprees, sexual risks or making foolish investments.

The extreme depressive feelings according to the Mayo Clinic include:

- Depressed mood, such as feeling sad, empty, hopeless, or tearful (in children and teens, depressed mood can appear as irritability)
- Marked loss of interest or feeling no pleasure in all or almost all activities

- Significant weight loss when not dieting, weight gain, or decrease or increase in appetite (in children, failure to gain weight as expected can be a sign of depression)
- Either insomnia or sleeping too much
- Either restlessness or slowed behavior
- Fatigue or loss of energy
- Feelings of worthlessness or excessive or inappropriate guilt
- Decreased ability to think or concentrate, or indecisiveness.
- Thinking about death, planning, or attempting suicide

Dr. Heaton's 2006 paper mentioned 31 episodes of fainting or near-fainting found in Shakespeare's works. As fainting in Shakespeare is from 'strong emotion' and not because of dehydration or blood on the stage, it could be an indication of "mania" as fainting is a manic symptom.

Interestingly, we see fainting in Shakespeare's two long poems. For example, in *The Rape of Lucrece* we hear: "Even manly Hector faints, here Troilus 'sounds'." Luc.1486. (The word "sounds" means "to faint.") And in *Venus & Adonis* the goddess Venus says:

Didst thou not mark my face? was it not white? Sawst thou not signs of fear lurk in mine eye? Grew I not faint? and fell I not downright?

Ven.643-645.

Shakespeare's plays are full of melancholic characters too, such as Timon of Athens, Malvolio, Lear, Jacques, Aaron, MacBeth, and Antonio. What is interesting is that the author never tells us *why* these characters feel so despondent. For example, in *The Merchant of Venice*, Antonio tells us "In sooth, I know not why I am so sad."

Most people assume Antonio is worried about his ships, but he claims they are not the reason for his depression. He says he has diversified his fortune; he has no family to share his emotions with, he is not in love, and he is not melancholy about losing Bassanio to Portia. Like someone with chronic depression, Antonio simply knows not why he feels sad.

Finally, a friend of mine who is bipolar asked this question in a group text: Does anyone else start physically shaking so hard when you are feeling extremely stressed out about something?

Although two people answered "Yes" another person answered as follows:

I used to start physically shaking and even crying when I was younger, but I learned to control it, so now when I feel a shaking episode coming on, I steel myself, so I no longer shake or cry.

I was curious to see if any of William Shakespeare's characters ever started shaking physically when they were feeling stressed out but discovered that shaking is often used when a character is fearful or in love.

- In *Othello*, "He supped at my house, but I therefore shake not."
- *Troilus and Cressida*: "You shake my lord at something. Will you go?"
- *As You Like It*: Orlando says, "I am he that is so love-shaked, I pray you tell me your remedy."
- *Anthony & Cleopatra* "Shake though to look on it. Get thee back to Caesar."

Thinking about Edward de Vere made me wonder if he too "shaked" when he had an epileptic fit. If so, did his friends tease him and call him "Shakes-Vere"? By the way, in the old days, people were told to put something like a spoon in the mouth of the epileptic person to stop him from swallowing his tongue. (This is an old wife's tale and is no longer encouraged.)

Biographers of Edward de Vere emphasize his hyper-sexuality, his wild buying sprees, and his impulsive business decisions. (He spent $70 million dollars in less than ten years.) One biographer pointed to Edward's hypochondriacal nature making it seem like he was faking feeling ill. Oxford called-in sick for extended periods of time, often acted restless, suffered from insomnia, and feelings of worthlessness. With that in mind, let us view his boyhood poem again. Might he really be talking about his bipolar disorder symptoms when he wrote these lines?

> Framed in the front of forlorn hope, past all recovery,
> I stayless stand to abide the shock of shame and infamy.
> My life through lingering long is lodged,
> in lair of loathsome ways,
> My death delayed to keep from life,
> the harm of hapless days;
> My spirits, my heart,
> my wit and force,
> in deep distress are drowned,
> The only loss of my good name,
> is of these griefs the ground.

The question to ask is this: did the same person who wrote *Loss of My Good Name* pen these morose lines when he was older?

> When, in disgrace with fortune and men's eyes,
> I all alone beweep my outcast state,
> And trouble deaf heaven with my bootless cries,
> And look upon myself and curse my fate,
> Wishing me like to one more rich in hope

A Brief Recap

The number of people worldwide living with bipolar disorder is approximately .06% of the population. In the United States, the number is closer to .03%. However, the combination of pediatric epilepsy and adult bipolar disorder (like that of the "real" author of the Shakespeare canon) is extremely rare. It occurs in approximately 20% of people who live with bipolar disorder. Or about **0.0006** of the U.S. population.

Sources

Below is a list of the plays, poems, and sonnets where the word death is found. Compliments of www.shakespeareswords.com.

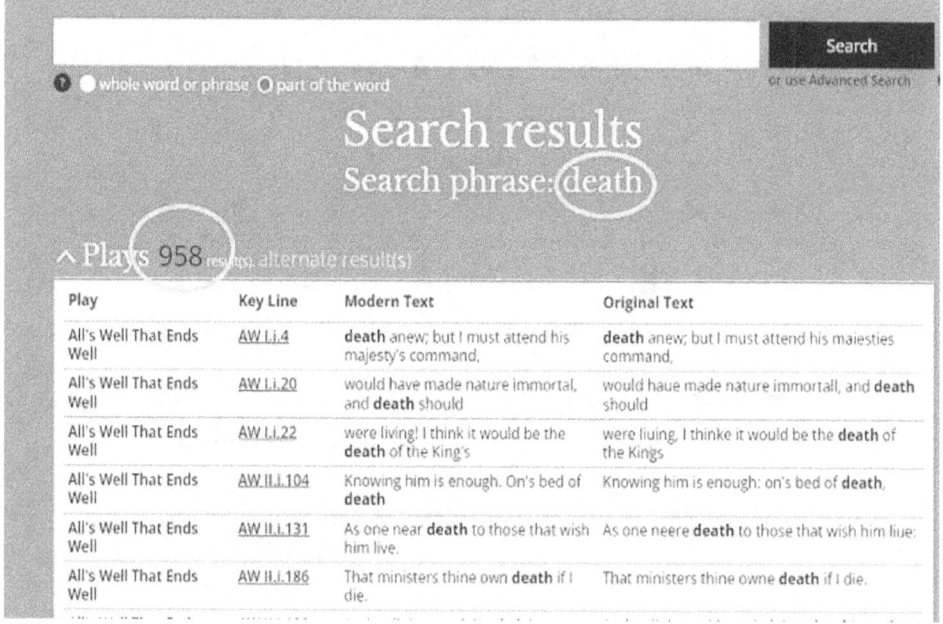

THE MYSTERY OF SHAKESPEARE'S LOST YEARS

List of Fainting from Dr. Ken Heaton's Article

Play or poem and reference*	Character fainting	Emotion and its cause
Two Gentleman of Verona 5.4.84	Julia	Grief at lover's betrayal
2 Henry VI 3.2.32	King Henry	Grief at uncle's murder
3 Henry VI 1.3.9	Rutland (child)	Fear of being murdered
3 Henry VI 5.5.43	Queen Margaret	Grief at son's stabbing
Venus and Adonis, line 645	Venus†	Fear of Adonis' being gored
2 Henry IV 4.3.111	King Henry	Joy at defeat of rebels
Romeo and Juliet 3.2.56	Nurse†	Horror at Tybalt's bloody corpse
Much Ado About Nothing 4.1.107	Hero	Shock at father's threatening to stab her
Julius Caesar 1.2.245	Julius Caesar†‡	Excitement at offer of crown
As You Like It 4.3.155	Rosalind	Horror at seeing Orlando's blood
Othello 4.1.41	Othello§	Horror at Desdemona's "infidelity"
King Lear 4.6.41	Gloucester	Belief that he had fallen off a cliff
King Lear 5.3.217	Kent†	Grief at Lear's madness
Antony and Cleopatra 4.16.70	Cleopatra	Grief at Antony's "suicide"
Pericles 22.34	Thaisa	Joy at reunion with husband
The Winter's Tale 3.2.144	Hermione	Grief at son's death
The Winter's Tale 5.2.80	Onlookers†	Grief at Hermione's death
Cymbeline 4.2.334	Imogen	Horror at finding headless corpse wearing husband's clothes

*Plays are listed in order of composition. References (act, scene, line) are to the Norton Shakespeare.§

†Faint off stage.

‡Probably grand mal epilepsy; described as foaming at mouth, "falling sickness."

§Possibly grand mal epilepsy; called such by Iago; also occurred the day before.

16

The Tempest Myth

Real-life mysteries on TV often flip the script. Just when you think you know the killer's identity, some new information will arrive that will question what you do know or send you off in a different direction. When it comes to Oxford, experts will die on this hill. They will claim, "There is no way Oxford could have written *The Tempest* because Shakespeare himself could not have written it prior to 1610. Period. This is conclusive proof Edward de Vere did not write the Shakespeare canon because he died in 1604. Dead men cannot write. End of story."

The phrase "conclusive proof" indicates finality. There is *no doubt* about it. But in this chapter, I want to use *The Tempest* as an example to flip the script and show the "tunnel vision" involved. Like police investigators who focus on one theory or suspect, and inadvertently block out all other possibilities, there is evidence that all the plays attributed to William Shakespeare could have been written before 1604. Thus, Oxford could be the author.

Let us start by looking at the *irrefutable* proof that Shakespeare wrote the play in 1610. It's called the Strachey letter. The story goes like this:

In June 1609, William Strachey set sail for Virginia on a ship called The Sea Venture, when a tempest, i.e., a hurricane, caused the ship to run aground on an uninhabited island in the Bermudas. Strachey described this place as "Devils islands" that were to be "feared and avoided ... above any other place in the world". Strachey and the ship's crew were stuck there for nearly a year. They were eventually able to construct two boats, which allowed them to continue their journey to Virginia. Strachey wrote an account of the shipwreck and "the precarious state of the settlement at Jamestown" in a letter that was suppressed by the Virginia Colony.

Strachey's letter was eventually published in 1625 as a newspaper article. It had a long title: "A true repertory of the wreck, and redemption of Sir Thomas Gates Knight; upon, and from the Islands of the Bermudas: his coming to Virginia, and the estate of that Colony then, and after, under the government of the Lord La Warre, July 15, 1610." The newspaper article was not printed until 1625, but a few pages of Strachey's account *may have* circulated in England in 1610. Someone may have sent them to Shakespeare.

So, what is the conclusive proof that William Shakespeare wrote *The Tempest* in 1610 and not prior to 1604? William "may have" seen a version of Strachey's letter before it was published in 1625. That is it. He *may have* seen a letter

Wait. This is the same William Shakespeare *who never received one single letter* from *anyone* except for somebody asking for money. But he "may have" seen the Strachey letter in 1610? Does this not seem more like speculation than irrefutable evidence? Yet Shakespeare-lovers make it sound like there is direct video evidence of William Shakespeare reading this letter in 1610.

Were there any other recorded accounts of a shipwreck? Or one that might suggest *The Tempest* could have been written prior to 1604? Yes. In fact, there are several, and I will get to them in a minute because there is a German play that resembles *The Tempest*, and it was written about nine years earlier.

In 1595, a German playwright named Jakob Ayrer wrote a play called *The Beautiful Sidea* which some researchers believe may have used *The Tempest* as its blueprint.

How could this be?

According to author Albert Cohn, English actors had come to Germany in 1585, and two of the men, Will Kemp and Thomas Pope, were "not only acquainted with William Shakespeare but also stood on an intimate footing with him."

Why would English "comedians" be visiting Germany in 1585? The answer concerns Queen Elizabeth's lover, Robert Dudley, the earl of Leicester. Besides being on a mission for the Queen, Dudley sponsored a troop of actors too. He thought it would be a promising idea to bring them along on his trip to the Netherlands and Denmark as well as Germany. The idea was to spread Protestantism, as many of the plays performed in Germany were stories from the Bible which most German audiences would comprehend – even if they did not understand English. In between the acts, a variety show involving fencing, juggling, leaping, music, and vulgar behavior would take place provided by the comedians.

How does this relate to the authorship of *The Tempest*? Albert Cohn writes:

"Jakob Ayrer was not the inventor of [the Tempest], but he had either a legend or a play before him. A proof of this is to be found in the first act, where Leudegast says of Prince Ludoff: 'Duke Leupold so loves strife and brawl, that now he's challenged us to fall.' Yet, no Duke Leupold appears throughout the whole piece. It's always *Prince* Ludoff not *Duke* Leupold."

Cohn goes on to add: "the confusion of names can only be explained by the careless use of the original sources. Ayrer's dramatic compositions after a certain date were under this influence, and some have concluded that his original source may have been an English drama with the same subject."

According to its' title page, *The Beautiful Sidea* was written "circa

THE MYSTERY OF SHAKESPEARE'S LOST YEARS

1595". One conjecture is that it was based upon an old English piece now lost, which Ayrer made use of in *The Beautiful Sidea*. Did William Shakespeare use the same source as the German writer?

Researcher Denis Mc Carthy, who made the discoveries for Michael Blanding's book, *North by Shakespeare*, states that Thomas North wrote plays for the earl of Leicester, however, no such play like *The Tempest* written by Thomas North has ever been found.

What about Edward de Vere? A letter written by John Hatcher to Burghley in 1580 proves Oxford and his players were busy touring the English countryside performing plays in the 1580s. Did Oxford travel to Germany? We do not know.

Albert Cohn believed *The Beautiful Sidea* was inspired by an earlier version of *The Tempest*. Paraphrasing him, "There are too many coincidences and similarities to Shakespeare's play." And quoting him directly, "the affinity to *The Tempest* cannot be purely accidental." Cohn's book *Shakespeare in Germany* written in 1865 can now be found free online.

The Tempest involves a shipwreck so one early source for it could have been a book written in Latin by the Italian historian Peter Martyr d' Anghiera, who in 1511 may have been the first person to write about Bermuda. His book, *De Orbe Novo* (On the New World, 1530) describes the first contacts of Columbus arriving in Bermuda (which Columbus had named San Salvador) and a Native American chief in Cuba named Guancanagarix.

Peter Martyr d' Anghiera

Another early account of a shipwreck occurred on August 15, **1559**. At this time, the 570-ton flagship **Jesus** entered the harbor in what is today Pensacol, Florida. The Jesus, along with ten other ships, carried 1,500 people. The intention was to create the first European settlement in the

Americas. The Spanish viceroy in Mexico wrote to the king of Spain that the harbor was safe for Spanish ships to land and claimed, "the harbor is so secure that no wind can do them any damage." But on September 19, the winds strengthened into what the native Americans called a "hurakan".

During the night, there came from the north *a fierce tempest* blowing for 24 hours from all directions. Master Diego Lopez and his crew of 50 aboard the Jesus drowned as their ship sank.

Also lost in the 1559 hurricane was the 492 ½ ton ship, **The San Andreas,** loaded with an estimated crew of 33 under its master Alonso Moralio. The Spanish settlers were assisted by an Indigenous leader who helped them reach what is today known as Alabama, and then most of them returned to either Mexico, Cuba, or Spain.

I mention these events to prove there were earlier Spanish stories about tempests prior to 1610, and in this second instance, a Native American chief assisted the settlers. There is mention of a shipwreck called The San Andreas, which in English would be translated as the "Saint Andrew."

In *The Merchant of Venice*, Salerno tells us "The wealthy Andrew was docked in sand," meaning a ship named San Andres was shipwrecked. Therefore, the account of The San Andres shipwreck of 1559 proves *The Merchant of Venice* could have been written prior to 1596, doesn't it?

Returning to the German playwright, Jakob Ayrer, some of his other plays included lines from *Macbeth, Much Ado About Nothing,* and *Titus Andronicus* but Ayrer died in 1605. Therefore, is it not possible that Shakespeare's plays may have been written much earlier than experts have allowed? How else could Ayrer have written similar plays in German? Albert Cohn tells us:

Playwright Jakob Ayrer wrote almost exclusively after English models which had been brought to him by the English players and at the Courts of Cassel, Dresden, and Berlin, we have seen an English taste exercising a preponderating influence and subjects taken from English history represented on the stage.

A Brief Recap

Although Shakespeare-lovers insist that *The Tempest* could not have been written any earlier than 1610, the evidence is flimsy. Plus, evidence shows that other shipwrecks could have inspired the original account. Therefore, *The Tempest* may have been written prior to Oxford's death in 1604, and then amended later.

Sources

Shakespeare in Germany in the Sixteenth and Seventeenth Centuries: An Account of English Actors in Germany and the Netherlands, and of the Plays Performed by Them during the Same Period by Albert Cohn.

Another excellent article is *Variety Entertainment by Elizabethan Strolling Players* by Louis B. Wright found at https://www.jstor.org/stable/27703047

The links for the Luna expedition:
https://pages.uwf.edu/jworth/jw_spanfla_luna_fleet.html

https://www.americanheritage.com/shipwrecked-history-spanish-ships-found-pensacola-harbor#3

https://archive.org/details/firstthreeenglis00arberich/page/232/mode/2up?view=theater&q=Bermuda

The Adventures of Columbus:

https://archive.org/details/deorbenovoeightd01angh

Oxford in Germany: https://deveresociety.co.uk/edward-de-vere-as-shakespeare/chronology/

> Edward de Vere died in June 1604 before almost a third of the plays were first performed. You cannot write plays if you are dead.
>
> But the works of Chaucer, Jane Austen, Sylvia Plath, & Anne Frank all became famous after their deaths.

17

The Thomas North Mystery

A new theory explaining Shakespeare's authorship arrived on the scene in the book *North by Shakespeare: A Rogue Scholar's Quest for The Truth Behind The Bard's Work*. In it, author and investigative journalist Michael Blanding, and rogue scholar Dennis McCarthy proposed an original theory. They believe that William Shakespeare wrote the plays, but he adapted them from old source plays written by Sir Thomas North. Using software used to detect plagiarism, they assert (among other things) that the private journals belonging to Thomas North were also 'borrowed' by William Shakespeare, and were used word for word in his play *King John*. There are direct links found between North's published and unpublished writings in such plays as *Hamlet*, *Macbeth*, *Romeo and Juliet* and other plays too.

For this book we will only focus on how someone might have accessed Sir Thomas North's personal diary to plagiarize him word-for-word. To start, if William Shakespeare purchased North's journal and used it to write his plays, why would the diary still be in the hands of the North family? *North by Shakespeare* tells us William Shakespeare freely plagiarized North's private diary, but it never left the possession of the North family. (They are in possession of it today.) And what about the two long poems *Venus & Adonis* and *The Rape of Lucrece*? Were these and the sonnets also written by Thomas North?

Taking a Closer Look

Digging deeper, we must journey back to the year 1558. This is when the plagiarized account from Thomas North's personal journals were first written. In 1558, Thomas North had accompanied the English ambassador on a secret journey to Italy that had been financed by Queen "Bloody" Mary, who was the ruler before Queen Elizabeth. A staunch Catholic, Mary had sent a secret envoy to witness the coronation of the pope. Thomas North described the procession of cardinals in his secret journal which can be found in the play *King John* which Blanding and McCarthy exhibit as proof of North's "linguistic DNA".

Nowadays, North's secret journals are not so secret. They can be viewed online. They are found in a book called *A Calendar of State Papers*. But if the North family has a copy, how can they also be in the State Papers? Most likely, upon his return to England, North's journal would have been copied and submitted to the crown. It would have been read by the Queen or her ministers and then locked in a file cabinet titled "State Secrets" for safe keeping.

Who had access to these secret files? Answer: Queen Mary's secretary of state. His name was John Vere, the *father* of Edward de Vere. After John's death, Lord Burghley would be next to guard the vault, and Burghley would have kept these files at Cecil House.

Could a curious 13-year-old boy who lived at Cecil House have found the journals while snooping around? Perhaps he was keenly interested in knowing more about his father, but might Edward de Vere have discovered Sir Thomas North's secret diary and read it? Perhaps Oxford looked him up, as he too was interested in taking a journey to Italy.

Thomas North had started his career by translating *The Dial of Princess* which concerned the life story of the Roman governor, Marcus Aralias.

However, according to Thomas North's biographer, tongues wagged after North's version was published. North was accused of using a Spanish version to translate Dial because he had inadvertently left the

Spanish word "libro" in several places. "Libro" is the Spanish word for book. However, the cover of *The Dial of Princes* claims North's version was "Englished out of *the French*" so why wasn't the French word for book used?

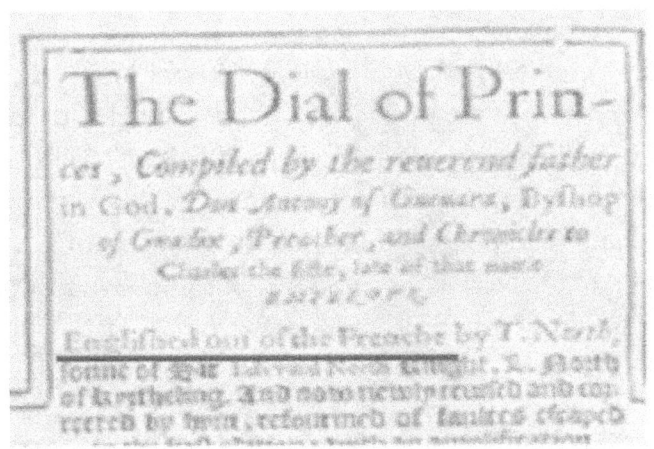

Dennis McCarthy claims Thomas North had purchased a copy of *Dial* for five shillings then signed and dated the back of it. So, according to Blanding and McCarthy, any changes made inside the book would have been made 100% by Thomas North and no one else. It makes sense, as North was planning to make revisions to the book's fourth edition.

But according to Kelly A. Quinn, in her article, "*Marginalia in The Dial of Princes*" for some mysterious reason, *none of the changes* found in Thomas North's personal copy of *Dial*, were ever used when the fourth, revised version of *Dial of Princes* was published in 1619. Instead, the editor relied upon revisions done by someone else who remains *anonymous*. Why? The initials of North's editor were A.M. which most experts believe was Anthony Munday. Who was Anthony Munday? He worked as Edward de Vere's secretary.

So, Thomas North was connected with Edward de Vere via Anthony Munday who had edited North's works before publishing them. My belief is Edward de Vere rewrote *The Dial of Princes* for Thomas

North for free, but if so, why would he do this? As mentioned earlier, most likely Oxford had been diagnosed with epilepsy as a child.

The Prince of Dials concerned the life of the Roman governor Marcus Aralias who also endured epilepsy. Also, another book I believe de Vere translated for North was *Plutarch's Lives*, again due to epilepsy. If Edward de Vere suffered from epilepsy, might he want others to be inspired by the lives of men like Julius Caesar, Hannibal the general who attacked Italy, Pythagoras, and Alexander the Great? All of them lived with epilepsy. Sir Thomas North got the credit for translating the French version of *Plutarch's Lives* by Jacques Amyot. To this day, North's version is called "Shakespeare's version", but I believe Edward de Vere acted as North's ghostwriter in both *The Dial of Princes* and *Plutarch's Lives*.

Edward de Vere had purchased the same French version of *Lives* written by Jacques Amyot. Oxford brought *Parallel Lives* with him on his grand tour of Italy in 1575 to 1576. So, did Edward de Vere help translate the version Thomas North published in 1580 without asking for credit? I would say "yes".

Yes, concludes Oxford researcher Stephanie Hughes. She claims a 25-year-old Edward de Vere might have very well been responsible for translating and editing *Plutarch's Lives* for Thomas North, because North was not as well-versed in Greek. Plus, in the two dedications of *Plutarch's Lives*, we find the word "love" used three times. Edward de Vere enjoyed using the word "love" but North? Not so much. So, would Thomas North use the word "love" three times in two brief dedications? Not likely.

Stephanie Hughes found both the Greek and the Latin version of *Plutarch's Lives* in the library of Sir Thomas Smith who was Edward de Vere's boyhood tutor. She claims it was not uncommon for tutors to require their students to translate passages from *Plutarch's Lives* from the original Greek to Latin and/or Latin to English as a homework assignment. So, if Edward de Vere had translated the Greek as a youth and then rewrote *Plutarch's Lives* for Thomas North, is this really a case of plagiarism? No. Oxford had originally transcribed the Greek passages for his first tutor Sir Thomas Smith, then gave them to Thomas North, and then he inserted them into the plays he attributed to Shakespeare. Technically, the only person who was plagiarized was Plutarch.

Oxfordian Gilbert Wesley Purdy also points out that even though Blanding and McCarthy claim that modern plagiarism software is foolproof, spelling back in the 1500's can throw this software a curve. The word honor for example might lead one to believe only one author wrote a passage, while "honour" could show several authors. View his blogspot and Facebook page for more information.

I use what I call "dictionology" which is a fancy way of saying that authors often use the same words over and over. Bottomline: McCarthy's "linguistic DNA" that proves Thomas North wrote the canon actually shows it was more than likely penned by Edward de Vere.

A Brief Recap

Living at Cecil House and spending time in the same household as Lord Burghley allowed Edward de Vere access to the skeletons hiding in the closet of Queen Elizabeth's family, as well as the personal journals of Thomas North. The "history" plays written by William Shakespeare tell the story of the Tudor family and explain the origins of the monarchy to the average Joe in a way that makes history come alive.

Oxford had also hired Anthony Munday to be his secretary. Munday worked to edit Sir Thomas North's books which allowed Munday with the means, the motive, and the opportunity to use anything written by Oxford.

Sources

Sir Thomas North's Marginalia in His "Dial of Princes" by Kelly A. Quinn: Marginalia in the Dial of Princes can be found at https://www.jstor.org/stable/24304350

Stephanie Hughes https://politicworm.com/oxford-shakespeare/the-argument/

Gilbert Wesley Purdy https://gilbertwesleypurdy.blogspot.com/

Most Scholars Claim Shakespeare Read Heliodorus a book that was dedicated to the earl of Oxford.

18

About Honor & Other Things

When I was 20 years old, my friend and I went to Europe, and I still vividly remember the day we took a ferry from Denmark to Sweden. The boat featured a fancy dining room where diners sat at tables attended by waiters. I had ordered fries and a sandwich, and when it arrived, I picked up the sandwich and took a bite. Suddenly it was like time froze, and the entire room became silent. You could hear a pin drop. I looked around. A woman pointed at me, her mouth agape. What was going on? Everyone seemed to be staring at me in disbelief. "Dude, put down the sandwich. You're supposed to eat it with a fork," my friend Warren hissed. The waiter arrived. "You are Americans?" he said with an accusatory tone. He wore a little smirk like a badge that showed he was clearly more refined than the two of us.

"Yes," Warren said casually. "Actually, we are from California, Hollywood to be exact". He showed the waiter his driver's license. Warren lived in North Hollywood which is about seven miles from where the celebs and rich people live. He also lived in the shittiest apartment in all of North Hollywood, but the guy looked at the two of us like we were rock stars. He suddenly seemed lost for words. As people in Texas say, "We were all hat and no cattle." Meaning we were bullshitting. We continued on with our lunch laughing about the incident when suddenly a voice over the intercom boomed, "Would the two nice men from Hollywood please enjoy some free strudel?" I mention this story to accentuate the word honor which was spelled "honour". Remember how the dedication for *Venus & Adonis* mentioned honor so many times? Narcissus claimed the boy lacked honor, but what did honor mean? To have honor meant possessing a nobleness of spirit. It was taught only to the wealthy, however, so a commoner would not know that an honorable individual had a duty to please the Queen and country first. An honorable person had a conscience and would never knowingly lie. So, if someone had never been taught a sense of honor it would be like using your fingers in a place where everyone uses a fork. For example, guess how many years William Shakespeare hoarded grain and resold it for a profit during years of a famine? 15 years. Was this an honorable thing to do? No. Scholars seem to forget about the important Elizabethan concept of honor but perhaps we can use it to help solve our cold case.

Like his father, William Shakespeare lent money when it was illegal to do so. Was this honorable? No. He also liked to sue people for small sums of money. Was this an honorable thing to do? Not for small amounts. People who were honorable were supposed to act Godly and adhere to the Christian values of patience and forgiveness. When William purchased a Coat of Arms for his father, allegedly for his dad being a successful grain merchant, was this honorable? Not really. An honorable gentleman would never lie, but William had stretched the truth about his father being a successful merchant. To Elizabethans, a coat of arms was a token of nobility. It allowed others to know that someone could be trusted at their word. Might the coveted symbol convince townspeople that William's father was not a crooked loan shark? After all, the emblem had been granted to John Shakespeare, not William Shakespeare?

Next, what about William's lack of musical knowledge? No one ever wrote about William Shakespeare playing a musical instrument and learning to play an instrument takes time and practice. Yet, according to author Joseph M. Ortiz, "music was a vital part of Shakespeare's theatrical practice…his characters frequently sing and quote popular ballads and songs. He tested various theories of music in complex and original ways." How could William do this if he had never learned how to play a musical instrument?

What about the lack of letters kept by others? Normally writers will jot down notes and/or mail letters to friends, spouses and even frenemies. Not William Shakespeare.. He worked 100 miles away from where his wife and children lived and wrote plays for twenty years. How many letters did his children keep? None. His neighbors did not even know Shakespeare was a writer. Nor did his wife.

Let me repeat that one. William Shakespeare was married for 34 years but his wife Agnes *never had a clue* he wrote 4 long poems, 37 plays and 154 sonnets. Please. If you happen to be married (like me) you will know how ridiculous this seems. It's like the guy whose wife came home holding her test results. Good news! It turned out she did not have Tourette's. She just effing hated him.

Likewise, maybe Agnes just effing hated William, so she burned everything. But why did it take two actors to compile his works to be published into the First Folio? A plaque and memorial statue stand in London to this day commemorating actors John Heminges and Henry Condell. It proves that Shakespeare's wife had no idea, how William made money. Does that sound believable?

In 1609 the sonnets were published, but the publisher dedicated the book to a dead person. The dedication reads to "our ever-living poet." Ever-living implies immortality, unless, of course, this was an anagram. An anagram is defined as "a word, phrase or name formed by rearranging the letters to form another word, such as cinema forms the word iceman."

So, "our ever-living poet" could be deciphered: to "our living poet Vere." Except this does not make sense if Edward de Vere died in 1604 – unless he faked his death and was hiding out in the forest like Robin Hood. (Let's not go there, shall we?)

Why dedicate the sonnets to an "ever-living" person if William

Shakespeare was still alive and kicking?

Looking for clues: we have no journals, diaries, play revisions or even household receipts that were kept by either William Shakespeare or his wife. This is strange. Even I keep receipts and jot down my personal thoughts and I am not much of a writer. My wife will vouch for this. She will even tell you; I have a bad writing habit.

My point is that for years it has been sacrilegious to doubt Shakespeare. Experts tell us he would NOT need to know anything about aristocrats, sword-fighting, dancing, law, botany, or anything else found in the Shakespeare plays. He could have researched these things at "ye-olde bookstore". Back then, yes, the printing press was like Google. It allowed people to open their minds and research things.

However, this is not altogether true. Elizabethan imaginations were limited by both the church and the government. Were people allowed to write that the earth revolved around the sun? No that was blasphemous. Could folks imagine that the stars were not fixed in the sky? No. If so, they would be burned at the stake as a heretic because the Bible said otherwise. To even "imagine the death of a monarch" was considered an act of treason punishable by death. But several rulers in the Shakespeare canon do die onstage, other monarchs croak offstage, so how did the "real" author know how to navigate this boundary without ever getting in trouble? Did he find that answer in a book? No. So William Shakespeare must have been close to the sovereign.

Did Queen Elizabeth ever lead William Shakespeare to believe that she liked him? No, it never happened. Instead, a letter from Gilbert Talbot to his father on May 13, 1573, reveals she was fond of Oxford.

"My Lord of Oxford (Edward de Vere) is lately grown into great credit, for the Queen's Majesty delighteth more in his personage and his dancing and valiantness than any other. I think Sussex doth back him all that he can; if it were not for his fickle head, he would pass any of them

shortly. My Lady Burghley (Edward de Vere's wife) unwisely has declared herself, as it were, jealous, which is come to the Queen's ear, whereat she has been not a little offended with her, but now she is reconciled again."

Queen Elizabeth liked Edward de Vere and displayed her affection for him in public, but there is no direct evidence proving Queen Elizabeth even knew Shakespeare. People vehemently disagree about the Queen having a child. But if it happened, would the queen freely admit to it? No. Never. In 1573, the future king of France had proposed to her which is why any talk of Elizabeth giving birth to a child out of wedlock was a serious national security matter. If someone like the Pope found out, he would call on Spain to launch an immediate attack on England. And on Edward de Vere's side, if Lord Burghley ever found out, he would have had Oxford's heart for lunch. De Vere was told to reconcile with his wife which he did. He told his wife he had made a mistake, and thought babies were born twelve months after conception, not nine months. It worked. Oxford and his wife got back together.

Finally, there is an adage about an apple not falling far from a tree. For all this talk about father and son, one quick look at William Shakespeare and Edward de Vere's lives shows us the similarities between father/guardian and son.

John Shakespeare	William Shakespeare
Wife was Illiterate	Wife was Illiterate
Liked to lend money	Liked to lend money
Liked to sue for lesser amounts	Liked to sue for lesser amounts
Invested in real estate	Invested in real estate
No record of schooling	No record of schooling

William Cecil	Edward de Vere
Book lover	Book lover
Cambridge Graduate	Cambridge Graduate
Master of Arts degree from Oxford University	Master of Arts degree from Oxford University
Latin expert	Latin expert
Honor was important	Honor was important

A Brief Recap

Shakespeare-lovers might disagree, but we don't know much about Shakespeare's life. In the next chapter, we will review what we do know.

Sources

Shakespeare Hoarded Grain:
https://historydaily.org/shakespeare-hoarded-grains-resold-profit-during-famine

Shakespeare portraits: http://www.shakespeare-online.com/faq/imagesofshakespeare.html

Was the Earl of Oxford Queen Elizabeth's Lover
http://www.anonymous-shakespeare.com/cms/index.268.0.1.html

Gilbert Talbot's letter: https://vgs-pbr-reviews.blogspot.com/2022/11/the-gossip-from-queen-elizabeths-court.html   Shakespeare evaded paying Taxes

19

Proof for William Shakespeare

Hollywood writers who pen mysteries are advised to "show don't tell" but when it comes to the authorship of William Shakespeare, this is hard to do. For example, what if a judge ruled that the name William Shakespeare found on the title pages of quartos and the First Folio was inadmissible? You could only prove the authorship by citing examples found in the works. Here are the four examples that are commonly used to prove that William's life intersects the poems, plays and sonnets:

1. **Hamlet.** William Shakespeare wrote *Hamlet* to honor his young son Hamnet, who passed away at the tender age of eleven in 1596. We are told that back then, spelling did not matter so Hamnet was the same as Hamlet.

2. **Sonnet 145.** Experts tell us that William's wife's name can be found in these lines: "I hate, from **hate away** she threw, **And** saved my life saying, "Not you." The word "And" certainly does sound like the name "Anne" but does "hate away" sound like "Hathaway"? No, but maybe it is a Midlander accent thing.

3. **Sonnet 135.** In this sonnet, William Shakespeare begs the dark lady to have sex with him, because back in Elizabethan times, a "Will" or "willie" meant a "penis" as well as "vagina", "desire," "willpower," "determination," and "choice" (free will) as well as the abbreviation of the name William. Here are the lines: *Whoever hath her wish, thou hast thy Will, and Will to boot, and Will in overplus, Wilt thou, whose will is large and spacious, not once vouchsafe to hide my will in thine.*

Many Shakespeare-lovers claim Will Shakespeare *must have* written this sonnet because the name Will is found in it. But his baptismal name was Guilielmus (a name still in use today). Therefore, shouldn't it be "thou hast thy Gill and Gill to boot and Gill in overplus?"

4. **All The Sonnets Together.** Researchers claim William used all the sonnets collectively to create a fictional story that interacted with his own life. This tale explained how he had fallen for a "dark" woman while traveling to and from his little village to London. Unfortunately, she already had feelings for another younger lover, so the two men fought as rivals for her affections.

Would these four examples convince anyone that William of Stratford upon Avon wrote all the sonnets, poems, and plays? No. Considering Shakespeare wrote 154 sonnets, 4 long poems, and 37 plays we would expect many more examples, wouldn't we?

What about those who claim William of Stratford was Prospero the nice guy from *The Tempest*? Prospero, we are told, resembles William Shakespeare because people believe that in real life William Shakespeare was convivial and a nice guy. However, we know Shakespeare hoarded grain, stiffed the tax collector, and sued people. His best friend John Combe was a loan shark (think Tony Soprano) and after he and William bought the tithes, they made the townspeople pay double what they had before. Not to burst your bubble, but perhaps William Shakespeare was not really a nice guy at all.

The other problem with Shakespeare's minimal attachment to the plays is that Francis Bacon or <name your candidate> can make the same claims as the Stratford man. He or she could have possessed a great imagination and have minimal attachment to the plays, poems, or sonnets too. For example, let's say Francis Bacon wrote the canon. He had a great education and if we look hard enough, just like the name "Will" in the sonnets, we could make a case for Bacon's name being found in some of the plays. The question is did Bacon write songs, or have an association with fainting, depression, and thoughts of death like his cousin Edward de Vere? No. However, as Oxford's cousin, (Bacon's mother was the sister of Mildred Cecil who was William Cecil's wife) Sir Francis Bacon would have been the logical choice to be the editor of the First Folio. Oxford's daughters may have hired him to do this.

When it comes to Edward de Vere, however, people have tried to keep Oxford's authorship a secret for more than 300 years. Why? Author Pete Frengel writes, "For generations a painting, known as 'The Ashbourne,' was identified as a portrait of William Shakespeare."

Then in the 1940s, Charles Barrell performed an X-ray analysis and discovered that the subject's forehead had been overpainted to better resemble the image of 'Shakespeare' on the First Folio, and that his ruff (collar) had been changed for that purpose as well. "Further analysis revealed that a coat of arms had been painted out, and that the date 1611 had been added, to correspond to the Stratford Man's age at that time – '47', as it says on the upper left inscription."

The Ashbourne

Frengle continues: "The Canadian Conservation Institute determined that the portrait was painted in 1597, the same year that Edward de Vere, the 17th Earl of Oxford was 47 years old. Interestingly, Charles Barrell concluded in *Scientific American* that the portrait was of

Oxford as well. So, why had the coat of arms been overpainted? It belonged to Elizabeth Trentham, the second wife of Edward de Vere the 17th Earl of Oxford."

Why the need to alter a painting?

Many Oxfordians have written about Edward de Vere's connections to the sonnets, but my own thought on them is this: when Oxford had traveled to Italy, he had stayed for two weeks at the home of the painter Titian who was renowned for his paintings of *Venus & Adonis* and *The Rape of Lucrece,* as well as making "self-portraits". Obviously to draw a self-portrait one needs a mirror, and that is how I view the sonnets: Oxford would look into a mirror and create 'word pictures' of himself at various times of his life. Also, two assistants helped Titian paint his masterpieces. Likewise, John Lyly and Anthony Munday were Oxford's two helpful assistants.

Regarding how Edward de Vere's life matches the Shakespeare canon, author Hank Whittemore has a wonderful website that offers over 100 examples. At least three plays by Shakespeare involve a husband like Oxford who blamed his innocent wife and then later regretted what he had done. Apparently, Oxford wrote about what he knew.

Finally, at least 13 plays attributed to William Shakespeare are set in Italy during the renaissance. This dovetails nicely with Oxford's trip to Italy in 1575. Most books make his journey seem like a frivolous, frat-boy, vacation, but Queen Elizabeth and her privy council had approved it. Oxford paid for the trip out of his own pocket, however, it may have involved him doing a bit of spying for her majesty as well.

At that time, the Arsenale di Venzia was known as the world's greatest shipbuilding facility. Located in Venice, Italy rumor had it that large numbers of men were building a massive number of ships.

THE MYSTERY OF SHAKESPEARE'S LOST YEARS

Back in Elizabethan times, it took about five years to build a Spanish galleon, but the buzz on the street said that at the Arsenale di Venzia, a ship could be built in half that time.

Records show that Oxford's main headquarters was in Venice (the star at the top) but he traveled as far south as Sicily which is the star located at the bottom.

In Palermo, Oxford met a young Spanish soldier named Miguel Cervantes, and because of his fluency with Spanish, Oxford later bragged of fighting with Cervantes and his Spanish commander Don Juan. Was this true or pure conjecture and braggadocio? We do not know. Over drinks with Cervantes, however, Oxford may have learned that 200 ships were being built for Spain to attack England. Might this not be important news to tell his Queen? (The Spanish Armada that eventually attacked England in 1588 consisted of about 150 ships.) As mentioned earlier, it took years to build a single ship, so it would make sense to have them built in Italy to decieve English spies communicating from Spain.

A Brief Recap

People have wondered for over 400 hundred years why the usually frugal Queen Elizabeth awarded Edward de Vere a lifetime pension of 1,000 pounds a year from her spy-paying account. To most scholars, Oxford was a ne'er-do-well who had done nothing to earn it. King James continued to pay his pension after he was crowned king, so did the Queen tell James that Oxford had earned it by spying for his country? Or was Oxford paid for writing the chronicles of the Tudor family in the Shakespeare history plays? What do you think?

Sources

A Calendar of State Papers Spain: https://www.british-history.ac.uk/cal-state-papers/simancas/vol4

http://www.oxford-shakespeare.com/BritishLibrary/BL_Add_28702.pdf

Charles Barrell who examined the portrait: https://prabook.com/web/charles.barrell/2501163

20

Final Thoughts

Most book mysteries end with an "aha" moment or a surprising twist. This "gotcha moment" will reveal truths about characters, answer the pressing questions, and will relate back to the beginning. Unfortunately, in real life things cannot always be summed up so neatly. At least not in this book. Yes, I believe that honor, music, and fainting help differentiate two different people, but my words will probably fall on deaf ears. However, my high school English teacher once taught me three rules about writing that she claimed applied to every writer.

Rule #1: Write what you know.

Rule #2: Rewrite often, it is the key to great writing.

Rule #3: Writing well is its own reward, but do not expect to get rich from it.

She *never* said, "The lone exception to these three rules is William Shakespeare." No, she said these rules applied to *everyone*, even Shakespeare. But when we do this, her advice seems to fall apart.

Applying the 3 Rules to William Shakespeare.

Rule #1: Write What You Know. William Shakespeare was a commoner, yet he wrote about aristocrats. He tested various theories of music in complex and original ways but did not know how to play a musical instrument. Fifteen of Shakespeare's plays take place in Italian or French locations, but he never once left England. People in his town knew him as the friend of a loan shark, John Combe, not someone who wrote plays. William Shakespeare failed to pay taxes, hoarded grain to resell during a famine, and raised the price for tithes. All these things were considered dishonorable. Ironically, he wrote an entire play, *Much Ado About Nothing,* concerning the importance of honor.

Rule #2: Rewrite Often, it is the Key to Great Writing.

What about rewriting? Within the strict time constraint of four years, William Shakespeare did not have time to rewrite seven plays, two 40-page poems plus a few sonnets while simultaneously acting in plays and studying the law. He lacked time for rewriting because during these same four years he was teaching himself how to read Latin. Oh, and reading several Latin books never translated into English.

In the First Folio actors Heminges and Condell claimed Shakespeare "never blotted a line," but why would they say this? William Shakespeare rarely signed his name, but on one of his signatures there is a huge blot. There is another blot on his second signature too. Therefore, to say he never blotted a single line is a bold-faced lie. Or this remark is 100% true *only if William Shakespeare never wrote a single line.*

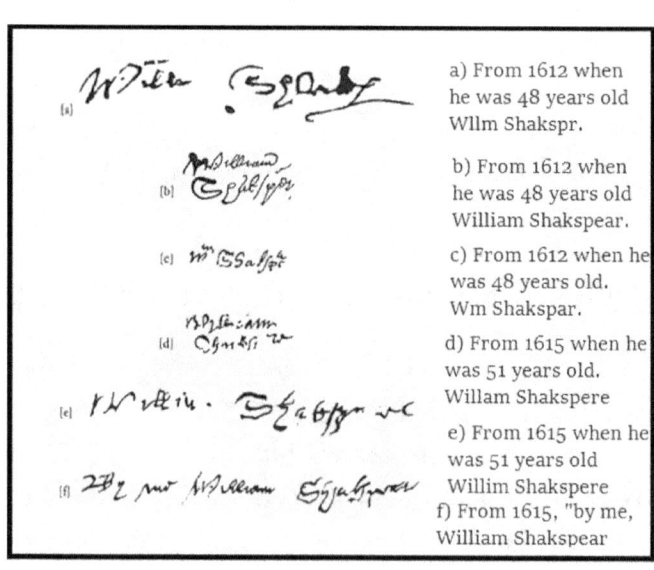

a) From 1612 when he was 48 years old Wllm Shakspr.

b) From 1612 when he was 48 years old William Shakspear.

c) From 1612 when he was 48 years old. Wm Shakspar.

d) From 1615 when he was 51 years old. Willam Shakspere

e) From 1615 when he was 51 years old Willim Shakspere

f) From 1615, "by me, William Shakspear

Rule #3: Writing Well is its Own Reward, Do Not Expect to Get Rich From it. Most actors claim, "You don't get into the theater, the theatre gets into you." Not William Shakespeare. After Oxford died in 1604, a few months later, William Shakespeare resigned from the Kingsmen. He turned his back on the theater and never acted again.

We are told that William Shakespeare wrote plays to "put butts in seats." He penned sonnets not necessarily to be biographical but to create a fictional story of the fair lady, the rival youth and himself. So, to put it politely, he wrote to fatten his wallet. He purchased real estate, a coat of arms, tithes, and the second-biggest house in town. Then he retired. This seems odd because normally we will see a movie star or singer who continues to perform waaaay past their prime. Why? Because they still crave the limelight, applause, and attention.

Shakespeare-lovers claim that anyone who disagrees with his authorship are snobs. People like me cannot accept the fact that someone from a lower class could write as well as an aristocrat. Not true. There are reasons to disagree with William Shakespeare's authorship that have nothing to do with snobbishness and more to do with common sense. Here are some examples:

1. **Easily Losing his Accent.** The video on *YouTube* shows an East Midlands guy who laughs because Londoners cannot understand his thick accent. We are supposed to believe that 400 years ago this was different. A Midlander could write seven plays, several sonnets, and two long poems without people wondering what he was saying. He *always* spoke with a Londoner's accent.

2. **The "Obscure" Poem *Narcissus*.** It came out in 1589 at a time when William Shakespeare was saving every penny to help rescue his mother's farm. He still would have purchased it. Right?

3. **Little Latin.** Ben Jonson claimed William knew "small" or "little" Latin, but Will would pay good money for an obscure poem written in Latin.

4. **Dr. Heaton's 2006 Fainting Study.** It shows that symptoms of fainting and a psychotic disorder show up in Shakespeare's plays, poems, and sonnets. There is no known cure today for bipolar disorder but the remedy for epilepsy shows up in the plays of William Shakespeare. Yet he never complained of depression, insomnia nor showed signs of any psychotic behavior.

5. **Signature Consistency**. The six signatures of William Shakespeare are not consistent. Either different people signed for him, or William was unfamiliar with using a pen. Does it make sense that a prolific writer would always sign his own name inconsistently?

6. **Honor.** The "real" author of Shakespeare wrote a dedication that mentioned honor seven times. The code of honor meant respect for God, Queen, and country. Yet William of Stratford hoarded grain and resold it for profit during a famine. Records show he regularly failed to pay taxes. And would an honorable man have more gold on his coat of arms than the Queen? No. Ben Jonson made fun of William's motto: Non Sanz Droict or "Not without Right." It was jokingly called by Jonson, "Not without Mustard," to poke fun at all the gold it had.

Shakespeare's Coat of Arms

Of course, "Not without right" could have been an anagram for "not outright with" (meaning this man is a concealer or "a beard" for someone else. A Shakes-beard.)

But nowadays, William Shakespeare is to Stratford upon Avon as Juliet is to Verona and who wants to spoil that? It is a big local money-maker, and it is not my intention to ruin that city's financial connection to Shakespeare or your love for Shakespeare's works either. So, why am I writing this book?

Edward de Vere was concerned about honor, not fame or recognition. As a scholar he was concerned with the truth. His last name, "Vere" is derived from "Veritas" the Latin word for "truth," so a more accurate name for the author of the canon should be **Shakes-Vere** as Edward de Vere wrote the works fronted by William Shakespeare.

Why is this so important if it happened over 400 years ago?

When people show a careless disregard for the truth it implies that the truth is not important or necessary. If a simple lie will effectively solve a problem, like Shakespeare's authorship, then it should be okay for everyone to lie. Convenience should be valued more than ethics. In this case, a noble person concerned with honor did not accept money or recognition for writing the canon. He honored his Queen and kept his word to her. He allowed his allonym to receive all the credit.

Today, scholars have used tunnel vision to address the authorship question. They state definitively that a correct conclusion has been drawn for their candidate. His name on the plays is the proof. But it's like someone who shoots at a barn and then paints a bullseye centered on the tightest cluster of hits. We are told, for example, *The Tempest must have* been written *after* 1610 because of Strachey's letter that "may have" been read by someone who never sent or received any letters. If you are still reading to this point, please tell me that I am not the only one who doubts this flimsy "evidence".

In 2006, British physician Dr. Ken Heaton studied every single poem, play, and sonnet and found a link between the works and fainting. Although the man from Stratford possessed no connection to fainting, it is listed as a symptom of both epilepsy and bipolar disorder. Edward de Vere's quirky personality traits included being a hypochondriac, (complaining of not feeling well often) excessive spending, sexual promiscuity, depression, and insomnia which are all symptoms of bipolar disorder. Experts of the past have shamed him.

Just to be clear though, there is no such thing as a "bipolar attack" like a fainting attack. A person with bipolar disorder experiences variations in moods over weeks, months, or years so the mood disorder is not something that comes on suddenly like a heart attack.

Oxford often expressed negative emotions as a young adult. He played a musical instrument and authored poems, or songs filled with tragic melancholy. These emotions match the depressed feelings also found in the writings of William Shakespeare. Both men openly complained of depression, had trouble sleeping, and they expressed feelings of worthlessness. They both penned songs and enjoyed music.

The Queen's Coat of Arms

It is these connections between the two men that add up to my belief that William Shakespeare served as an allonym for the playwright, songwriter, and poet, Edward de Vere. Does another candidate including William Shakespeare of Stratford upon Avon match these symptoms? No, nor does Sir Francis Bacon.

THE MYSTERY OF SHAKESPEARE'S LOST YEARS

Bipolar Symptom	"Real" Author	William of Stratford	Edward de Vere	Others
Melancholic	✓	—	✓	—
Can't Sleep	✓	—	✓	—
Feeling of Worthless	✓	—	✓	—
In Despair	✓	—	✓	—
Wrote Songs	✓	—	✓	—

Not long ago, I was standing in line at the supermarket, and the woman in front of me had her daughter sitting shoeless in a shopping cart. While waiting in line Mom counted the toes of her daughter, singing loudly, "This little piggy went to the market, and this little piggy stayed home. This little piggy got roast beef and this little piggy had none, and this little piggy went, 'wee, wee, wee, wee, wee, wee' all the way home." When she finished, they both laughed and then the daughter innocently asked, "Mommy, which market did the first little piggy go to?" The mother looked back at her and said, "Wal-Mart" and then she and the cashier had a hearty laugh.

But it made me think. Mom may not have realized that "this little piggy went to market" *meant slaughtering the pig*. Taking the pig to market was code for selling it.

During the reign of Queen Elizabeth, people often communicated in code. It was considered an act of treason for a Catholic priest to hear a confession, so the average person had to be concerned about saying or writing something publicly that might get them into trouble. Assassination plots on the Queen were common. Every year there was someone new who wanted to be the next ruler of England.

The "Essex Rebellion" of 1601, for example, was one such power grab. It involved roughly 100 men who had ridden into London with its two leaders to wrest the crown from Queen Elizabeth. The idea was that Queen Elizabeth was too old (she died in 1603) and had not yet named a successor. If she were to go to the Globe Theater to watch *Richard II* written by William Shakespeare, with a new scene added where the king publicly surrendered his throne, then perhaps she might follow its example. Maybe she would be willing to step down if put on the spot in public.

Robert Devereux, the earl of Essex would be there to swoop in if the Queen did step down. He would be named her rightful successor. Essex stated his first order of business would be to get rid of Robert Cecil, the son of Lord Burghley.

The Queen did watch *Richard II* with the new scene and clearly, she did get the message. However, she ordered her soldiers to arrest the conspirators, charge them with treason and jail them.

Who were the "brains" behind the Essex Rebellion? Robert Devereux, Henry Wriothesley, and William **Shakespeare**. Devereux received three whacks to the back of his neck from an axe, which eventually beheaded him. Henry Wriothesley received a life sentence in the Tower of London but was later released from prison by King James. And William **Shakespeare**?

Even though **Shakespeare** may have acted in the play and should have been severely punished for writing the new scene, Queen Elizabeth *did not even question him.*

Remember how after *The Rape of Lucrece* she may have promised not to harm Edward de Vere or his allonym? The Queen kept her word, however as the saying goes, "revenge is a dish best serve cold." Perhaps she told Robert Cecil: "Promise me that you will bury Edward de Vere's name after I am dead."

THE MYSTERY OF SHAKESPEARE'S LOST YEARS

Let us try to sum things up regarding Shakespeare's two sets of lost years. Written evidence indicates that William **Shakespeare** lived on a farm at Ingon Meadow with his parents from birth to his marriage when he was 18 years old. He and his wife and children may have moved to the farm of his brother-in-law in Shottery after his marriage. What about the second set of years from 1589 to 1594? Hold that thought.

Not long ago, I watched a *Dateline* episode where a killer who lived in Southern California failed to show up for a court hearing and skipped bail. The killer had lots of money so when police searched for him, they went to his last known whereabouts in Santa Barbara. He had been staying at his father's house and numerous deleted Google searches were found on his father's computer that mentioned "cheap apartments in Alberta and Quebec" so the police were confident he "must be" in Canada.

It never crossed their minds that the killer who owned a house less than 100 miles from the Mexican border might try to trick them and go to Mexico. Five years later, when the case went cold, the cops received a call from Mexican police. The man had been arrested in Southern Mexico after the airing of a "Unsolved Mysteries" TV show. He had been living in Mexico the whole time.

Similarly, we have an unsolved mystery where people have hunted all over England to find out where William Shakespeare might have gone during his "lost years" of 1589 to 1594.

But like the police in Southern California who never looked for the killer in the most obvious place, **Shakespeare** -searchers have been thrown off the scent by the phrase "shake a scene." Most people assume William **Shakespeare** was acting in plays during this time.

Yes, William may have walked to London in Feb 1591 and stayed with printer Richard Field, someone he knew from his village, for a brief time. But, after receiving money from Oxford or his attorney in 1592 for the use of his name, he was told to "lie low." What did he do?

Shakespeare lent out money to John Clayton in London before he returned to Shottery to stay with his wife and their children at her brother's farmhouse. The proof Agnes and William Shakespeare had stayed in Shottery is that she owed money to a shepherd named Thomas Wittington who named both William and Anne Shakespeare as debtors in his will.

But not a shred of evidence exists for William **Shakespeare** *acting* in a group of players from 1592 to 1594. According to Edward Alleyn's papers at Dulwich College, the second performance of *Harry VI* was made on March 6, 1592, and the players mentioned are Richard Burbage, John Duke, Augustine Phillips, Thomas Pope, George Bryan, and Robert Pallant. All of them would be future Lord Chamberlain's Men. But the name William Shakespeare was not found as a player in 1592.

Another document dated May 6, 1593, is a license from the Privy Council to travel during the 1593 plague epidemic. The actors mentioned include Edward Alleyn as servant of the Lord Admiral and five men who belonged to Lord Strange's Men: William Kemp, Thomas Pope, John Heminges, Augustine Phillips, and George Bryan. Again, no William Shakespeare.

What about the Queen's paylist for performances for the last week of December 1594? Yes, the name William Shakespeare shows up, but the money was not paid out until March of 1595 which does not actually prove he acted in the plays. William **Shakespeare** may have been just the money man. He may have fronted the salaries for the Christmas performances and asked for his name to be added to the paylist so he could be recompensed.

What about Greene's Groatworth of Wit? Doesn't this pamphlet reference William Shakespeare in the line about "shakes a scene"? Possibly. But could not "shakes a scene" apply to *any* actor who shouted or was talking excessively loudly? Interestingly, William Shakespeare retired from the Kings Men acting company in 1604, the same year that Edward de Vere passed away.

The First Folio was published in 1623 and was dedicated to two men: William Herbert and his brother Phillip Herbert. They were both multi-millionaires which is important if you believe in the police-show adage "follow the money". If we do this with William Shakespeare, we find a dead end. The First Folio was published after the death of Shakespeare's wife and there were 750 copies printed. This would have cost a pretty penny; however, the two Herbert brothers could have easily afforded it. What was their connection to Oxford's family? Phillip Herbert was married to Susan Vere, Oxford's daughter, and William Herbert was engaged to marry Bridget Vere, Oxford's youngest daughter, but the marriage did not go through. Most likely the two sisters inherited the plays, poems, and sonnets when their stepmother Elizabeth Trentham passed away in 1609, which is the year the sonnets were printed.

Let us revisit the three rules of writing I learned in high school and apply them to Edward de Vere.

Applying the 3 Rules to Edward de Vere.

Rule #1: Write What You Know. Edward de Vere grew up close to Queen Elizabeth, and personally knew dukes, lords, and ladies. Oxford was a royal ward who composed songs and love poetry at the Elizabethan court. He played a musical instrument, traveled widely across the European continent, and lived for over one year in Italy. Using push pins on a map of Italy, the cities where he stayed matches the places found in the Shakespeare canon. To honor his boyhood choir master Richard Edwards, he included the lyrics from Edward's song Griping Grief in *Romeo and Juliet*. While married, Oxford had an affair with Anne Vavasour, one of the Queen's ladies in waiting, whose olive complexion was considered "dark" and not 'fair-skinned.' Therefore, his mistress had a dark complexion matching the "dark woman" of Shakespeare's sonnets. These are just a few instances, but one good example of how the life of Edward de Vere intersects the Shakespeare canon is that Bertram in *As You Like It* was also a royal ward whose legal guardian chose his wife. Bottomline: Edward de Vere wrote about what he knew.

Rule #2: Rewrite Often it is the Key to Great Writing. Unlike William Shakespeare, Oxford had no severe time constraints. He penned his first play before the age of sixteen with Richard Edwards. Later, he held a lease on Blackfriar's Theatre and supported two players groups: The Oxford Boys and The Oxford Men. The play, *The Comedy of Errors* was first performed by a children's group in 1577 and then rewritten for the law students at Gray's Inn in 1594, proving that rewriting is the key to great writing.

Rule #3: Writing Well is its Own Reward, Do Not Expect to Get Rich From it. The American author Kurt Vonnegut lived life with bipolar disorder and claimed that writing each day helped him feel better. So, it makes sense why Oxford might need to write daily too. It was not to get rich. He wrote to vent his bipolar thoughts, but he could never shake his feelings of melancholy, worthlessness, and need for sleep. We find these same things in the Shakespeare canon. Like Kurt Vonnegut, writing helped Oxford feel better.

On the flip side, William Shakespeare has always come off as a supernatural being. His writing skill, arising from his own supernatural brilliance, appeals to some people because he never had to work at it. Writing came naturally and his genius did not need a teacher to prove himself to the world. For this reason, Shakespeare is the patron saint of kids who hate school and having to study. He is an inspiration for students who claim they don't need an education to make it big in life. If William **Shakespeare** did not have to study, why should I?

Most people love the story of the natural born genius from a small town who showed up the rich, snobbish, college elitists. It sells better than a story about a temperamental, flawed human like Oxford who was intense but suffered from mood swings. (So did Steve Jobs). Or someone today on the same level would be Elon Musk, who is also self-confessed as bipolar.

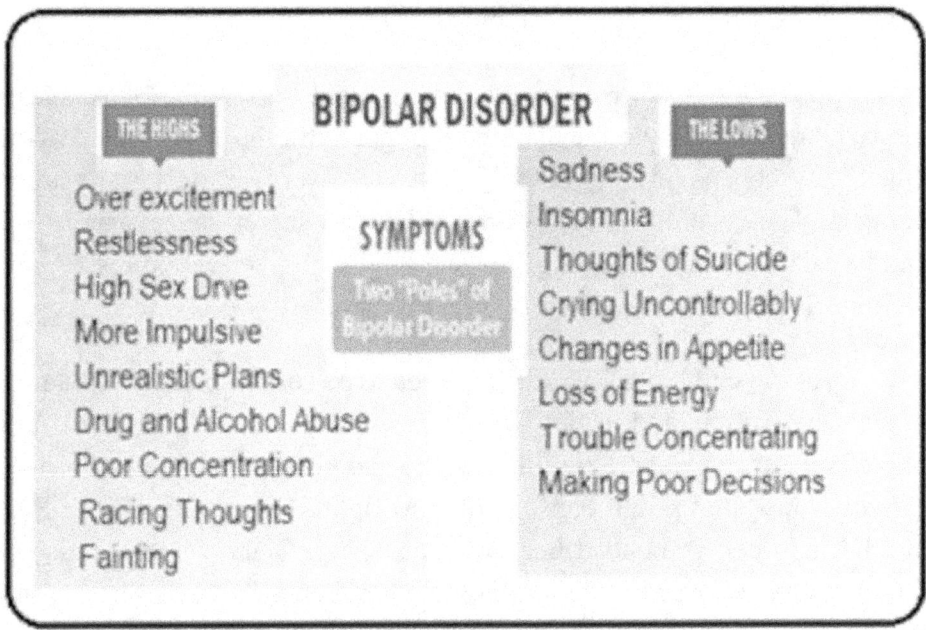

My goal for this book was to explore Shakespeare's lost years. As we asked "why" Shakespeare would bother to answer *Narcissus*, we started to expose the myths, mysteries, and mistakes of what experts have told us about William Shakespeare's life and times. Solving this 400-year-old cold case means changing how we look at the man named Shakespeare.

However, I am also a realist. I do not expect any words of mine to convince you of anything. You might be as lazy as me and decide the juice is not worth the squeeze.

I understand how you feel, and many people have felt like you, however, what we have found is that no one ever got fired for changing his or her beliefs about who wrote the Shakespeare canon. Do a little research on your own and decide for yourself. Use the internet to assist you.

If you are an instructor, have fun with this book. I challenge you to have your students fact-check me.

The man who wrote the plays attributed to William Shakespeare offered an alternative to the average playgoer who had only heard about kings and queens in fairytales. His royals were mortals, not super-humans. They were not always nice, but his secret sauce was to put emotional truth in everything he wrote. His characters expressed real feelings and emotions because he too felt them.

However, Queen Elizabeth wanted to be certain that her reputation as a strong woman and leader would remain intact, even after her death. She could not risk people finding out she had been raped and had birthed a son because that might cause people to fight. After all, if Queen Bess had been forced to behead her own half-sister, Mary Queen of Scotts, might others be forced to do this too? Robert Cecil, the son of her trusted advisor was given the job of making certain that Edward de Vere's connection to Queen Elizabeth got squashed. Robert Cecil had no problem burying his brother-in-law's name because Oxford had acted indifferently when his sister had died.

But the truth has a funny way of coming out no matter how hard anyone tries to hide it or stop it. Edward de Vere changed people's lives because he dared to speak his truth. Therefore, his plays, poems, songs, and sonnets were autobiographical and in them, he revealed his true self, and his battle with depression, thoughts of suicide, and death. The words, "To be or not to be" is about self-harm, isn't it? Might Oxford have had assistance with writing the plays? Certainly, but like the painter Titian, who also used assistants, Edward de Vere threw his own voice and thoughts into the works. Doing so, he subconsciously inserted his struggles with depression, as well as explain his affection for Elizabeth and fears for Henry Wriothesley who was imprisoned in the tower of London. He might have been like a "guncle" to him. (A gay uncle) The sonnets tell this story and now that you know what to look for, you will find Oxford there. The sonnets might make more sense now if seen as being biographical.

If interested, use the resources in this book to learn more about this story.

Finally, in our household, when we say goodbye it is done with a hug and a kiss. It is with this same sentiment that I thank you for taking your valuable time to read this book. I truly do appreciate it. Que le vaya bien. (Be well.)

This is a new Shakespeare Stamp from the Netherlands

RESOURCES

Shakespeare and Italy

https://hankwhittemore.com/reason-number-24-why-edward-de-vere-was-shakespeare-his-deep-knowledge-of-italy/

Shakespeare and Music:
https://www.gutenberg.org/files/19676/19676-h/19676-h.htm#DESCRIPTION_OF_FRONTISPIECE

Bipolar Disorder in Epilepsy

On_the_prevalence_of_bipolar_disorder_in20160623-21552-1pe0qop-libre.pdf

The 140 volumes of Abe Urbe Condita by Livy
https://harvardreview.org/content/livy-alive/

Shakespeare and the Law
https://shakespeareoxfordfellowship.org/shakespeares-bad-law/

Sacred Geometry and Shakespeare
https://www.facebook.com/robertedwardgrant/videos/349825325698102/

Helen Gordon: Dedication to Shakespeare's Sonnets Is a Love Story

The Shakespeare Authorship Coalition: https://doubtaboutwill.org/

Don't Quill the Messenger Podcast:
https://www.dragonwagonradio.com/dontquillthemessenger

Shakespeare and Music

https://doi.org/10.1093/acrefore/9780190201098.013.1190

Heraldry Laws: https://www.heraldica.org/topics/britain/england2.htm

Gilbert Wesley Purdy https://gilbertwesleypurdy.blogspot.com/

ABOUT THE AUTHOR

A graduate of UCLA with a BA in English literature, Robert Boog lives in Santa Clarita, California. His hobbies include sleeping, taking long walks to the refrigerator and petting his dogs. He and his wife Roxana own a small real estate company.

Robert Boog

www.ingramcontent.com/pod-product-compliance
Lightning Source LLC
Chambersburg PA
CBHW072047290426
44110CB00014B/1583